"I love this book! The compelling [stories of God's intervention] into unlikely lives inspired me, en[couraged] me to continue sharing His mes[sage. It is] a book of hope and promise, of unexpected encounters and transformed lives, of Divine appointments and extraordinary outcomes. Let God use it to soften your heart toward Him and others."

Lee Strobel, Bestselling Author of *The Case for Christ* and *The Case for Grace*

"'Irresistible grace' is a theological expression high on the ladder of abstraction, but *Compelled* makes the reality clear with seven stories that many readers will find irresistible."

Marvin Olasky, Executive Editor of News & Global, *Christianity Today*

"*Compelled* is a gripping, powerful, faith-inspiring page-turner that showcases how God uses all things, no matter how hopeless they may seem, for the good of those who love Him and are called according to His purpose."

Ginger Hubbard, Bestselling Author of *Don't Make Me Count to Three* and *I Can't Believe You Just Said That*

"There's nothing like stories of God's transforming power at work to inspire, encourage, and challenge us! In *Compelled*, Paul and Sarah Hastings have gathered a thrilling collection of real-life testimonies that showcase the redeeming work of Jesus. Read these incredible stories and be reminded that no situation is too tough, no life too broken, for His grace to redeem and restore."

Andy Bannister, Director of Solas Centre for Public Christianity (Scotland)

COMPELLED

COMPELLED

ORDINARY PEOPLE
EXTRAORDINARY GOD

PAUL & SARAH HASTINGS
WITH ELLIE PAYNE

10 Publishing
a division of 10 of those.com

Unless otherwise stated, Scripture quotations are from The Holy Bible, English Standard Version, ESV®. Text Edition: 2016. Copyright © 2001 by Crossway Bibles, a publishing ministry of Good News Publishers. Used by permission. All rights reserved.

Scripture quotations marked CSB have been taken from the Christian Standard Bible®, Copyright © 2017 by Holman Bible Publishers. Used by permission. Christian Standard Bible® and CSB® are federally registered trademarks of Holman Bible Publishers.

Copyright © 2025 by Paul & Sarah Hastings

The right of Paul & Sarah Hastings to be identified as the Authors of this Work has been asserted by them in accordance with the Copyright, Designs and Patents Act 1988.

All rights reserved. No part of this publication may be reproduced, stored in a retrieval system or transmitted in any form or by any means, electronic, mechanical, photocopying, recording or otherwise, without the prior permission of the publisher or the Copyright Licensing Agency.

British Library Cataloguing in Publication Data
A record for this book is available from the British Library

ISBN: 978-1-83728-054-4

Designed and typeset by Pete Barnsley (CreativeHoot.com)

Printed in Denmark

10Publishing, a division of 10ofthose.com
Unit C, Tomlinson Road, Leyland, PR25 2DY, England

info@10ofthose.com
www.10ofthose.com

1 3 5 7 10 8 6 4 2

Dedicated to our parents:
Pat & Ganya Hastings
Ken & Julie Axmann
Jon & Lory Payne
who taught us to love Christian testimonies

CONTENTS

Introduction: Compelled | 1

1. Falsely Accused and Sentenced to Life in Prison | 5
Hannah Overton

2. Among Cannibals and Headhunters | 27
Don & Carol Richardson

3. Transgendered to Transformed | 41
Laura Perry Smalts

4. Miracle at the Pentagon | 59
Brian Birdwell

5. Abortion Clinic Owner Reborn | 73
Carol Everett

6. Church Boy | 93
Troy Gause

7. A Double Life | 107
Jeff Parker

Conclusion | 125

Contributors | 131

INTRODUCTION:
COMPELLED

If you ask a child about their favorite part of the Bible you'll never hear them mention the 23rd Psalm, or Paul's letter to the Romans, or Jesus' Sermon on the Mount. Instead, you'll hear them clamor for the story of Noah's Ark, Moses and the Red Sea, David and Goliath, or Daniel and the Lion's Den.

Jesus Himself was a masterful storyteller, using parables to convey spiritual truths to His audience. Case in point, the entire Bible begins as a story in Genesis, "In the beginning…"

For me, stories were a formative part of my life, especially Christian biographies. I remember saving my money as a child so I could buy illustrated books about missionary pioneers like David Livingstone and Hudson Taylor. I paid $1.50 for each title, knowing I could resell them for $0.50 and buy even more biographies.

Eventually, I discovered more modern testimonies like *God's Smuggler* by Brother Andrew, *The Hiding Place* by Corrie ten Boom, and *The Cross and the Switchblade* by David Wilkerson. The stories always jumped off the pages, whether they involved smuggling Bibles behind the Iron Curtain or trekking into Africa to shine the light of the gospel.

But the common thread behind all of these stories was Jesus.

The God who became a man, just so He could die for a broken world and make all things new. It was greater than any stage play and wilder than any science fiction novel. But most incredibly… it was a *true* story.

A story that has compelled millions of ordinary people to exhibit extraordinary faith. To leave behind their comfortable lives and minister to lepers. To contract malaria and typhoid so that others may know Him. To risk life and limb and even walk into the Roman Colosseum facing certain death.

In 2018, my wife and I harnessed this lifelong passion for stories and launched the *Compelled* podcast; a quest to uncover some of the most powerful testimonies of lives that have been transformed by Jesus.

Through the podcast, we've met believers from every age, background, ethnicity, and socioeconomic status who have seen God work in remarkable ways. The seven stories you now hold in your hand are just a handful of those unique encounters.

You'll meet a mother who was falsely accused of murder and sentenced to life in prison; you'll travel deep into the jungles of New Guinea and live with a tribe of Stone Age cannibals; and you'll fall into a blazing inferno wrought by the devastation of September 11, 2001.

But in each of these true stories, you'll come face to face with the One who can set captives free, give sight to the blind, and make dead hearts alive.

Our prayer is that these stories would reassure you of the incredible power of Christ and kindle fresh affection in your heart for the Author of your own story.

—*Paul Hastings*

"For the love of Christ compels us, since we have reached this conclusion, that one died for all, and therefore all died. And he died for all so that those who live should no longer live for themselves, but for the one who died for them and was raised."

2 Corinthians 5:14–15 (CSB)

1

FALSELY ACCUSED AND SENTENCED TO LIFE IN PRISON

HANNAH OVERTON

Hannah sat in the courtroom, stunned and trembling, as the hum of voices rose to a fever pitch. But nothing could drown out the one word still echoing in her mind after the crack of the gavel: *Guilty.*

Accused of murder, tried, convicted, and now sentenced to spend the rest of her life in prison.

God, how could You let this happen?

Hannah's heart pounded with fear and anguish, and she buried her face in the arms of her husband, Larry. Weeping uncontrollably, she closed stinging eyes on triumphant prosecutors, stone-faced jury members, and eager reporters snapping pictures.

Police officers surrounded Hannah, pulling her up and handcuffing her wrists behind her back. As she was led from the courtroom, hot tears rolled down Hannah's cheeks at the fresh realization that she would never again be allowed physical contact with her five precious children, the youngest only seven months and still nursing.

How is Larry going to explain to them when he goes back home… alone? How will he tell them that their mama isn't ever coming back?

Hannah's tears turned from heartbroken to bewildered.

Why, Lord? I've seen You work wonders for Your people so many times… I'm innocent, and all You had to do was reveal the truth! Why didn't You? Where were You?

***

One year earlier…

"I'm home!"

Hannah closed the front door behind her and knelt to receive the four grinning children racing down the hall, clamoring for hugs. She put her arms around all of them, then glanced back down the hallway. Peeking around the corner, she saw a pair of bright blue eyes, longingly watching the little group. Hannah smiled and held out an arm.

"You want hugs, Andrew?"

Around the corner bounded a little four-year-old boy, grinning from ear to ear and eyes sparkling. His tiny feet flew across the floor, and he wrapped his arms around Hannah.

"Love you… Mommy."

Tears welled up in Hannah's eyes as she heard the name "Mommy," and she squeezed Andrew tightly.

Little Andrew had already experienced a great deal of hardship in his young life; he never knew his father, and his mother was a drug addict, which resulted in Andrew being born addicted to multiple substances. Due to his abusive home environment, Andrew was placed in foster care. When Hannah's daughters met Andrew at church, Hannah's tender heart had gone out to him.

Now, as Andrew ran off to play with the other kids, Hannah stood slowly, a hand on her pregnant belly and brushing at her eyes.

Thank the Lord he's with us now… in a few months, the adoption will make him officially part of our forever family, just like he's been praying for. It already feels like this is where he belongs…

***

"Mommy, my head hurts… and I feel cold."

Hannah laid a hand on Andrew's forehead as he stood looking up at her. It had been five months since Andrew moved in, and he was unusually listless this afternoon.

"All right, buddy… let's get you to bed, and see if you feel better after some rest."

Soon after, Andrew began vomiting, and pregnant Hannah sighed.

Must be a stomach bug…

A few hours later, Hannah peeked into Andrew's room, to see the little boy curled up in the corner of his bed.

Good, he's asleep…

But as she looked again, Hannah's heart dropped to her feet. The rise and fall of Andrew's back was irregular; he wasn't breathing normally.

Hannah and Larry raced Andrew to the nearest urgent care, where they were quickly transferred to a nearby hospital. By the time they arrived, Andrew was in a coma.

Thousands of prayers were offered up for Andrew that day, by friends, family, and others, the most desperate pleas coming from Hannah and Larry, as their precious son faded. Doctors were running tests, but didn't have any immediate answers.

Please God, please, heal him, please…

Later that night, Hannah lifted her head from Larry's shoulder, rubbing her eyes. She glanced down at her phone to see a text from a friend, sharing a Scripture. Hannah read it eagerly, desperate for any encouragement or glimmer of hope.

> *"Commit your way to the LORD; trust in him, and he will act. He will bring forth your righteousness as the light, and your justice as the noonday."*
>
> Psalm 37:5–6

Hannah dropped her phone back into her purse, confused.

What does that have to do with anything? God, I want You to heal my son… that verse means nothing to me right now.

An hour later, Hannah heard her phone buzz again. It was another text message from a different friend sharing a Scripture. For the second time on that nightmarish day, Psalm 37:5–6 appeared on Hannah's phone screen.

God, what are You trying to tell me? This verse says nothing about healing or comfort…

A few minutes later, Hannah was startled as the door to the hospital room was flung open. Two police officers entered.

"Mrs. Overton?"

"Yes?"

"We're sorry, ma'am, but you need to come with us. You're wanted down at the station for questioning."

Hannah blinked. "I don't understand."

The officer coolly replied, "We just need to get some facts straight."

***

Hannah clasped her hands to keep them from shaking as she sat in the stark interrogation room. A police officer dropped several medical papers on the table.

"Mrs. Overton, these are the results of Andrew's tests. As you can see, an astonishing amount of sodium was found in his blood. Ma'am, have you ever tried to intentionally hurt Andrew?"

The officer looked knowingly at Hannah.

Hannah stared up at the officer, confused.

"Sir… my husband and I have never once tried to harm any of our children, including Andrew. Why are you asking?"

The officer looked at her grimly.

"Tests don't lie, ma'am."

***

Hours later, Andrew died—just 30 hours after they had arrived at the hospital. Hannah felt as though someone had reached in and crushed her heart. The little boy who had wandered into their lives and captured their love was gone. Hannah sat in silent shock, unable to process what had happened.

What she and everyone else wouldn't find out until much later was that Andrew had suffered from a rare medical condition called hypernatremia, which results in high concentrations of sodium in the blood. Andrew had also been suffering from pica, an extremely rare, undiagnosed eating disorder, which gives victims an insatiable appetite, sometimes even causing them to crave non-food substances such as paint, glue, or baking soda.

On the day prior to his death, Andrew had most likely found and eaten a large quantity of table salt, which in addition to his body's propensity to high sodium levels, caused him to die of salt poisoning.

At the time, however, all Hannah knew was that her baby boy had died. But her nightmare was about to become even worse... Shortly after Andrew's passing, the District Attorney's office began promoting their own theory as to the cause of his death.

Hannah's story began appearing all over the media and on every local newspaper headline.

"PREGNANT MOTHER MURDERS FOSTER SON... Hannah Overton force-fed four-year-old son 23 tablespoons of chili seasoning... purposely neglected to take him to ER sooner, hoping to cause his death... will stand trial..."

Hannah felt like her world had been turned upside down.

Why is everyone acting like I'm guilty? It's like they've already decided...

But there was one hope that Hannah clung to.

That bag of Andrew's vomit that they saved in the urgent care... once it's tested as evidence it'll prove my story.

But as months passed, the urgent care's bag of evidence could not be found.

And so, Hannah was put on trial for capital murder.

***

Months later, the week of the jury trial came, and nothing went in Hannah's favor. The media ate up every detail, the local community was divided, and depictions of Hannah as an abusive mother, murdering her son in cold blood, could be found all over the news.

Throughout the trial, it became increasingly clear that Hannah had not force-fed Andrew anything, as the story presented by the media and prosecutors suggested.

However, the prosecution doubled down, continuing to malign Hannah as guilty.

"Any loving mother," the District Attorney pointed at Hannah, "would have sought medical help sooner. However, Mrs. Overton did not, because she wanted her foster son dead."

The world's leading nephrologist, a doctor specializing in salt-poisoning cases, was present at the trial, waiting to testify.

Hannah absently rocked her seven-month-old daughter in the car seat at her feet, as she scanned the crowded courtroom.

She whispered to Larry, "Why hasn't Dr. Moritz been allowed to testify yet? He told me that if he'd been in my shoes, he would have done the same things we did. Surely he'll clear up all the confusion the District Attorney is creating! But it's been three days now, and he still hasn't been called up to testify…"

Due to multiple delays and odd behavior on the part of the District Attorney, Dr. Moritz never ended up giving his crucial testimony to the jury. Similarly, another doctor who had previously known about Andrew's eating disorder waited for five days to share his testimony with the court, but was never called up.

***

At last, after months of interrogations, deliberation, and media speculation, the verdict was to be given. Hannah, strained and exhausted, sat impatiently waiting for the judge to announce the jury's "not guilty" verdict so her life could return to normal.

Everyone stood for the verdict.

Then, Hannah's whole world fell apart.

She stood paralyzed, unable to breathe; every word from the judge's mouth seemed to be squeezing her lungs.

"Guilty as charged... life sentence... no chance of parole... all physical contact with children forbidden..."

Hannah had walked into the courtroom a free woman, fully expecting to be vindicated; instead, she was led out of the courtroom in handcuffs, a convicted murderer.

As she was surrounded by police officers, and pulled from Larry, Hannah's mind sped back to that morning when she had kissed her five children goodbye, not knowing that she would never again be allowed physical contact with them. And her baby, barely seven months old, would wake up in a few hours and cry for her mother, whose touch she would never feel again.

I never... never thought I could actually be found guilty...

Hannah was taken from the courthouse to the county jail and locked away in solitary confinement to await her transfer to prison.

For the next few days, alone in the small cell, she cried out to God, lost and hopeless.

I trusted You to save the day... and You didn't.

***

Days turned into weeks, and finally, Hannah felt she couldn't go on. She was in emotional turmoil, unable to eat, and terrified of sleep; her nights were plagued by horrifying nightmares, such as her children drowning in a submerged car out of her reach.

One night, Hannah was being escorted down the darkened hallway in the jail, on her way to make one of her few midnight calls to Larry.

I can't live like this any longer… I'm going to die.

Hannah wasn't planning to end her own life; she simply didn't think she would live any longer, separated from everyone she loved so dearly.

Earlier that night, Larry had found their eight-year-old son, Isaac, crying. "I can't do this anymore, Dad. How can I live without Mama?"

Larry was silent; then, he handed Isaac his Bible, his voice rough with tears. "Read this, son… I'll be right back."

Larry went into the garage, laid his head against a shelf, and sobbed. When he finally pulled himself together enough to re-enter Isaac's room, Larry found his son no longer crying, but smiling.

"Daddy, Daddy, look!" Isaac pointed enthusiastically to Philippians 4:13 in the Bible. "It says right here that 'I can do all things through Christ who strengthens me'! We can do this, Dad… you need to tell Mama when she calls tonight!"

Isaac didn't know how much Hannah needed to hear about his faith that night, but God knew, and He used that promise to sustain Hannah and her family through the many trying years ahead.

Another evening, lying in bed, Hannah was complaining to God about her surroundings.

All I see every day are concrete walls, steel bars, this ugly jumpsuit, and only one tiny window. And all I can see through that is a "No Parking" sign!

As she drifted off, she thought miserably, *I don't even get to see the flowers...* The next morning when Hannah awoke, she stood, stretched, then walked over to her small, sixth-floor window. She was stunned by what she saw: arranged on the "No Parking" sign was a colorful bouquet of blossoms.

What in the world...

Hannah couldn't believe her eyes. In the middle of the night before, a friend, feeling urged by God, had bought the bouquet and arranged it on the sign, not realizing it was the only sliver of the world Hannah could see from her cell.

Hannah slid to her knees on the floor, tears spilling down her face, as she felt her Father's love rush over her.

OK Lord... I hear You. I still don't understand any of this... but I'm going to try to trust You.

Psalm 37 flashed through Hannah's mind—the verses her friends had sent her when Andrew was in the hospital.

Trust in him, and he will act. He will bring forth your righteousness as the light, and your justice as the noonday.

Hannah sighed.

I know You can, Lord... but will You?

***

As Hannah emerged from the prison van, handcuffed and surrounded by guards, her nervous gaze was met by the hollow eyes of hardened, angry women. The past few weeks in the county jail felt like ill preparation for spending the remainder of her life in prison.

One inmate, upon seeing Hannah, started shrieking, "Fresh meat! Fresh meat!" Hannah felt small and scared as she was escorted to her dorm. The moment she stepped in, she was assaulted by the rank smell of women who hadn't used shampoo or deodorant in years; few could afford such luxuries, and with no air conditioning in the summer, the heat and stench were oppressive.

Worse yet, Hannah was only allowed to see Larry once a week during brief visits and only from opposite sides of a table. She saw her children even less frequently, about once a month, and only from behind bulletproof glass.

One day, Hannah was sitting alone in the prison yard, staring up at the cement walls blocking out the blue sky. The faces of Hannah's children flashed across her mind, and she began to cry softly.

Hannah didn't notice when a side door opened and Sheryl*[1] appeared. Sheryl was a fellow prisoner assigned to train Hannah for her inmate duties and was also the leader of a Wiccan circle, an occult group that practiced witchcraft.

Looking at Hannah, Sheryl's face contorted angrily; she stormed up to the bench and said furiously, "Overton, are you crying *again*? What is your problem?"

---

1 Throughout the book, names followed by an asterisk have been changed to protect the person's identity. All other information remains faithful to the actual events and circumstances.

Sheryl's language turned foul as Hannah stared up at her, eyes still wet with tears. After a long string of profanity, Sheryl snapped, "Why can't you just grow up? This place is your home now, you gotta just accept that."

Hannah stood up defiantly and said fiercely, "This will *never* be my home."

Sheryl let out a harsh laugh and responded mockingly, "Oh yes it is! And you better get used to it, crybaby, or you'll never survive!"

Hannah opened her mouth, then closed it again.

Sheryl continued cursing angrily, "This is where you get your mail, right?"

Hannah hesitated for a moment, before replying meekly, "Yes."

"And this is where you sleep, right?"

"Well, yeah."

"Then this is your home!"

Hannah remained silent.

Sheryl continued in a slightly calmer tone, "You say you believe in God, right?"

Hannah nodded and Sheryl resumed, "Well, if there really is a God out there, like you say, then He's put you here for a reason… and that would make this place your home! So either you believe in Him or you don't."

All Hannah could do was turn and walk away. That night, she sat on her bed, still indignant and upset from the encounter. She picked up her Bible and aimlessly let the pages fall open on her lap. Her eyes fell on Acts 17:26–27.

> *"And he made from one man every nation of mankind to live on all the face of the earth, having determined allotted periods and the boundaries of their dwelling place, that they should seek God, and perhaps feel their way toward him and find him. Yet he is actually not far from each one of us…"*

The boundaries of their dwelling place…

Hannah set down her Bible, overcome.

God is the one who determines my dwelling place, and right now, as much as I may not understand it, He's put me in this prison. Sheryl may have been unkind… but she was right… If I say I believe in God, I have to trust Him.

It was a small change, a shift in Hannah's heart, but it was the spark of faith she needed to believe that God was good and would give her the grace to live in contentment where He had placed her.

And so, Hannah began to adjust to her new life, not just enduring it, but seeking to thrive in it, and looking for ways to share her hope with fellow inmates. When she took her eyes off her own pain, God opened them to the pain of the women around her: drug addicts, prostitutes, women wrestling with guilt, those who had been abused, others in angry denial or deep depression.

One thing led to another, and a simple conversation with another prisoner about Jesus' love quickly turned into a regular Bible study with a handful of other inmates. It wasn't long before the number of women who wanted to participate in the Bible study exceeded the maximum group size allowed in the prison, so more Bible study groups were formed.

The change that had started in one woman's heart spread like wildfire, and soon women all over the prison began finding their hope in Jesus. God had done the redemptive work that only He could do; He had taken Hannah's horrible trial and brought about more good than anyone could have imagined possible.

***

Walking down the dim corridor to her dorm, Hannah was about to turn the corner, when she was startled by a shadow. She jumped and began trembling violently.

It's Katy*, it has to be... this is it, I know it, my time's come...

Katy was another inmate, whose girlfriend had recently begun attending Hannah's Bible studies. Katy was worried that Hannah would advise her girlfriend to end their relationship, and she had decided the only way to fix the problem was to get rid of Hannah.

Hannah closed her eyes, shaking with terror, her mind racing back to that horrible day a few weeks ago, when Katy had threatened to take her life.

Ever since that day, Hannah had lived in constant fear, expecting Katy to jump from the shadows with an improvised weapon at any moment.

Hannah jerked back to the present and peeked around the corner... and breathed a sigh of relief to see that there was no Katy; the shadow had been her imagination.

A few weeks later, Hannah was shocked to walk into her dorm to see several prison guards leading Katy away in handcuffs. Hannah's newfound friend Marcy* hurried over, grabbing Hannah by the shoulders.

"Hannah, they found Katy's hidden weapon! I told you we wouldn't let anything happen to you… They figured out her plan, and she's going into solitary confinement!" Marcy grinned. "I can't believe I got to see the whole thing… pretty wild!"

Hannah felt relief wash over her.

Thank you, Lord, for Your protection…

But as Hannah lay in her bed that night, she felt troubled as she pondered Marcy's morbid excitement over the whole ordeal, something that had been mirrored by many of the other women.

How have these women become like this, so hardened, so bloodthirsty?

Then came a chilling thought… *What if I become like that? God, how can I keep from becoming like these women here in prison? They're so bitter…*

Immediately Hannah received a clear answer: *Forgive.*

But, forgive who, Lord?

The answer made Hannah's stomach turn: *The assistant prosecutor from your jury trial.*

Surely not, Lord!

This assistant prosecutor, a woman named Rachel*, had repeated wrongful accusations against Hannah and had fought hard to put her in prison for life; certainly, God couldn't expect Hannah to forgive her. *Besides,* Hannah thought, *she doesn't deserve forgiveness.*

Then Hannah felt the Lord say gently, *You're right, My child, she doesn't. But neither do you.*

At that moment, Hannah knew exactly what God wanted her to do.

Write a letter of forgiveness to Rachel.

Hannah recoiled at the thought.

Absolutely not. I'll forgive her in my heart, but I'm not going to write her a letter.

For weeks Hannah resisted, but eventually, the prompting from God grew so strong that Hannah surrendered. Everything inside of her hated what she was doing, but Hannah dutifully scrawled out the words she believed God wanted her to communicate to Rachel.

There, that's done. Hannah breathed a sigh of relief.

Mail the letter. The Holy Spirit's direction was unmistakable in Hannah's mind and heart.

Hannah hesitated. *I did what God told me to do, didn't I? I wrote the letter… that's good enough.*

Hannah tucked the letter away, out of sight, and tried hard to forget it.

God, I've forgiven her in my heart. That's what matters, so I don't need to send this.

Eventually, Hannah tore up the letter. But, after more weeks of resisting, Hannah finally relented. She wrote out a final letter to Rachel, saying she was placing Rachel's case in a higher court—God's court—and that the all-knowing God of Truth would ultimately give the ruling on Rachel's actions. Hannah quoted from the story of Joseph and shared that although she had been treated unjustly, God had used it for good. Women were joining Bible studies all over the prison and broken lives were being healed by Christ. After sealing the envelope and writing the address, Hannah hesitated, then finally dropped it into the outgoing mail.

Rachel's just been promoted to District Attorney... she probably won't even receive a letter from a convicted felon, let alone read it...

Yet God knew exactly what He was doing. Rachel not only received Hannah's letter, but read it and was greatly moved. She showed up at Hannah's pastor's office in tears, and soon afterward became a Christian. Because of her position as the new District Attorney, she had the power to allow Hannah's lawyer to review the evidence from Hannah's trial again.

And so began the process of God bringing Hannah's righteousness to light. The bag of evidence from Andrew's vomit that had been missing for years was finally found. Incredibly, it had already been tested, proving Hannah's innocence, but was then hidden by the lead prosecutor.

The world's leading nephrologist, as well as the doctor who had treated Andrew before his death, were finally able to give their crucial testimonies. As a result of all the new evidence, the Texas Court of Criminal Appeals agreed to reopen the case.

Months passed. Hannah was sitting in her dorm preparing for a Bible study when she received the message. She could hardly believe what she was reading; her case had been overturned and all charges had been dropped. She wanted to get up and dance and shout with joy, but instead, she read and reread the words, tears running down her face.

"Thank you, Jesus," she cried as she knelt beside her bed. Hannah had finally begun her journey home.

But the light Hannah had brought to the prison would not leave with her. Countless women had been saved as a result of Hannah's witness. Katy, the woman who tried to take Hannah's life, had surrendered her life to Christ and had begun attending Bible studies. Sheryl, the Wiccan leader who had constantly harassed Hannah, had also been saved. Countless other women had repented and become Christians as a result of Hannah's outreach. Over 100 women were now participating in the Bible studies, with groups being led by the new converts Hannah had discipled.

Into one of the darkest corners of society, God had brought light, through one woman with a faith that could not be locked in.

***

Hannah trembled with nervous excitement as she stepped into the hushed courtroom, the same room where the gavel had fallen and shattered her life so long ago.

As the magistrate went through some preliminary opening statements, Hannah almost bounced on the edge of her seat, smiling ear to ear.

At last, the judge signed the final papers and handed them to the bailiff. She reached down to shake Hannah's hand, and Hannah saw tears glistening in the judge's eyes as she said, "Congratulations, Mrs. Overton. You're a free woman."

After seven years and seven months in prison, Hannah was finally free.

Hannah's reunion with her children was one of the sweetest moments of her entire life. As she gathered them into her arms and kissed their upturned faces, Hannah shed tears that were both sorrowful and overjoyed.

Emma, only seven months when Hannah had been taken, was now a vivacious eight-year-old. Hannah mourned the years she lost; yet she was also full of joy for the years still to come, surrounded by her children, whom she had been told she could never touch again.

***

Since Hannah's exoneration and release in 2014, Hannah and Larry have founded Syndeo Ministries, which distributes Bible studies, encouraging letters, personal toiletry items, and cooling towels to hundreds of incarcerated women across Texas, and even provides housing for those who are recently released.

Hannah understands that these women need care for their imprisoned bodies, but even more importantly, they need to be told how they can be set free in soul. The Bible studies that Hannah started during her incarceration have since grown to include 1,000 prisoners, with another 10,000 inmates reached every summer and Christmas through Syndeo's special outreach programs.

Even while falsely accused and imprisoned, the Lord gave Hannah a passion to tell lost women about the Savior, the One who was also falsely accused, who chose a death sentence He didn't deserve to break the chains of fallen people, prisoners of sin, so that they could walk free, their ransoms paid and their shame taken away.

2

AMONG CANNIBALS AND HEADHUNTERS

DON & CAROL RICHARDSON

An orange sun set over the lonely island of New Guinea. Silhouetted against the fiery sky stood 200 Sawi warriors, holding drums, drawn bows, and spears.

Twenty-seven-year-old Don Richardson shifted in his canoe to look back at his wife, Carol, and seven-month-old son, then turned to face the throng of naked men.

Lord, You know we don't understand a word of their language, and all we want to do is to share Your good news and peace with these people… please help us.

***

Don and Carol Richardson met at Prairie Bible Institute in Alberta, Canada, in 1953. Don was from Canada, and

Carol was from the United States, yet both knew God was calling them to missionary life. The two eventually married, and in 1961, welcomed their first son, Steve.

One day, the Richardsons and a few of their friends attended a talk at their school by a visiting British speaker; the auditorium was full, and before long the young couple was spellbound by the passionate man on stage.

"Friends, in Romans 10:14–15 the Lord says, 'How then will they call on him in whom they have not believed? And how are they to believe in him of whom they have never heard? And how are they to hear without someone preaching? And how are they to preach unless they are sent?' Our call is to spread the gospel to 'every nation, tribe and tongue,' but we so often forget altogether about the lost souls on the other side of the world, who have never heard of Jesus or the Bible and are enslaved to sin with no hope of ransom."

Don and Carol leaned forward in their seats, eyes glued to the speaker.

"For example, near the equator, north of Australia lies the island of New Guinea, where hundreds of villages have been surveyed by military aircraft during World War II, but no contact with the outside world has ever been made."

The speaker looked up and seemed to be gazing right at Don and Carol.

"These souls are sinners in need of a Savior... but how will they accept Him if they don't even know He exists?"

***

The following year, in 1962, on a lonely river in New Guinea, a small group of dugout canoes glided through the murky waters. Don ran an arm over his dripping, sweat-soaked face, then turned around to smile tiredly at Carol, who sat holding little Steve, draped in a raincoat.

A few days before, Don and another missionary had journeyed together deep into the jungle to scope out their chosen place of ministry. They had selected a region they knew was inhabited by the Sawis, a people group which had never made contact with the modern world. It was also believed that the Sawis were headhunters and cannibals, ritualistically eating their slain enemies. But they were humans in need of a Savior nonetheless, and Don and Carol felt called to this people group.

During their expedition, the two men had encountered a small group of solitary Sawi men and through sign language agreed to trade some of their tools for the Sawis' help in building a small hut. After the work was done, Don headed back up the river, promising he would return to stay in this new home.

Now, as their canoe finally slid into the soft mud shore, Don looked up to survey his family's new mission field.

Casting sunset shadows, the silent throng of 200 Sawi warriors appeared pensive, and Don was unsure of their intentions.

Is this a welcome committee? Or will Carol and I become the Sawis' next meal? Lord, help us.

Breathing a quick prayer, Don jumped from the canoe, keenly aware of all the piercing eyes on him. In silence as tight as the bowstrings training arrows at him, Don reached to take baby Steve from Carol, then turned to walk ashore. Immediately, the warriors let out a startling wild cry, threw down their weapons and began running down to surround the newcomers.

Don did not realize that in Sawi culture, if a man entered a village carrying a baby, it was a sign that he had come in peace. God had placed His hand of protection over the Richardsons and had allowed Don to communicate peaceful intentions to them, without knowing a single word of their language.

Instantly, Sawi women and children materialized out of the jungle and joined the warriors in a wild chant, dancing around the Richardsons in rhythmic circles. Carol whispered to Don, "It's like being in the eye of a human hurricane!"

Later that evening, Don leaned against the door frame of his new home and looked out at the crowd, still dancing in the lingering twilight.

Well, Lord, You've brought us safely this far.

The Sawis danced and celebrated for three days and nights without stopping, demonstrating just how life-changing the Richardons' coming was for them. Through trading with nearby tribes, the Sawis had heard of the legendary "Tuans," fair-skinned people of great magical power who flew in giant birds in the sky, possessed medicine of great healing power, and wielded magical devices that could make voices travel through the air.

Now, Tuans had come to the Sawi people, and nearly 800 Sawis quickly moved in around the Richardsons' home. A meal didn't go by for the family without at least four or five curious faces pressed up against their window screens.

Being hunter-gatherers, the Sawis ate everything from wild pigs to grubs and bark, staples the Richardsons soon learned to dine on as well. Above all, the couple was determined to learn the Sawi language as quickly as possible, and thankfully, the Sawis were more than happy to help. With nine hours of daily language study, it didn't take long for Don and Carol to begin to converse.

All the while, as the family grew accustomed to jungle life, the couple was looking for opportunities to begin sharing the gospel with these lost people.

***

Crack. Crack. Crack.

An ominous rhythm resounded through the jungle, as Kamur village women began chanting and beating sticks against trees and the ground.

In the large clearing in front of the Richardsons' house, two rows of warriors holding bows and spears stood facing each other, one group from Kamur, and the other from the enemy village of Haenam. Both of these Sawi villages had uprooted and encamped around the Richardsons' home for months now, along with other Sawi villages, during an uneasy peace.

Don and Carol stood in their doorway, watching soberly. Carol groaned, exclaiming, "This is their fourteenth battle in two months! Why can't they just see that they're all Sawis and get along?"

Don sighed and dragged a hand through his hair. "A Haenam warrior killed a man from Kamur several years ago… and revenge is in the Sawis' blood. I've been begging the Kamur men to make peace, but they don't seem interested."

A battle chant broke out across the field, and Don turned to his wife. "We'd better start getting the bandages ready."

The warriors screamed and rushed at each other, letting spears and arrows fly. The peace of God seemed far, far away.

***

It was 1963, and Don sat cross-legged in the Sawi meeting hall, the fire casting flickering shadows on the Sawi men's faces, as they sat listening intently to Don's words.

"… now Jesus knew the time had come for Him to die. Judas, one of the disciples, betrayed Jesus, his friend, to the men who wanted to kill Him. And—"

Wild laughter erupted from the group, and Don stopped in confusion.

"Tell us more about Judas!" one Sawi called, and the grinning circle nodded in agreement. Another man, Kani, spoke up. "Judas, the traitor—he sounds like one of us. We can make one of our own tribe, or another tribe, trust us, and believe he is one of us... then we kill him!"

Kani gestured up at the rafters, where dozens of human skulls hung, brown and aged. "We can keep his head for a trophy, then we eat his flesh to absorb his spirit, to make us stronger!"

He thumped his chest, giving a gap-toothed smile. "Just like Judas, eh?"

As Don walked into the house later that night, Carol took one look at his face and knew she didn't have to ask how the meeting had gone. He dropped, exhausted, into a chair.

"I don't know what to do, Carol. It seems like these people will never understand the gospel. They live in fear of evil spirits, they kill and eat each other for power... they think Judas is the hero of the Bible and that treachery is the highest ideal!"

Carol sighed and set down her sewing.

"I know; I was teaching some of the women how to dress wounds this morning, and tried to explain their need for the Lord. They looked at me like I was crazy, and shook their heads; they're so afraid of evil spirits. They have no category for a loving God!"

Resting his head in his hands, Don nodded and let out a tired sigh. Carol picked up her Bible, flipping it open. After a moment, she read softly from Galatians 6:9, "And let us not grow weary of doing good, for in due season we will reap, if we do not give up."

She took her husband's hand, squeezing it gently. "That's us, Don... we *will* reap, if we don't give up. We can plant and water, but in the end, God will give the increase, and we have to trust Him for that. Even if we don't see it in our lifetime."

***

About a month later, as the hot morning sun slid over the village, Don was absorbed in some translation work when he heard the cries of men and women once again.

Not another battle...

But when he stepped outside, Don was confused by what he saw; scores of Sawis from all over Kamur were soberly gathering in the Richardsons' backyard. Men, women, and children from both tribes, all together, waiting.

Don spotted a young man, Ari, and called, "What's going on?"

Ari responded in a grave voice, "Tuan Don, you've been telling us to make peace with Haenam. You told us that if we didn't, you would have to go to another village. Our people have finally agreed; we will make peace."

Don was still very confused, but he followed Ari's gaze into the clearing and watched silently.

The people of Kamur stood on one side, facing the people of Haenam. Kaiyo, a Kamur warrior, came running forward, cradling his six-month-old baby son. Kaiyo's face was etched with grief as he ran through the Kamur throng, over the patch of open ground, and on toward the group of Haenam warriors. Behind him, Kaiyo's wife, Wumi, screamed and ran after him until she tripped and sprawled on the muddy ground where she lay sobbing, her face contorting in anguish while she screamed and cried, "Why must it be us? Others have many, and we only have one… why us? Why, why?"

Other Kamur women joined Wumi's wailing, as Kaiyo ran into the circle of Haenam warriors and stood face to face with the men who had tried to harm him on multiple occasions. After holding his son for one last moment, Kaiyo handed the baby over to the Haenam warriors. Solemnly, each of the Haenam warriors approached the child, one by one, placing their hands on the child.

Don whispered to Ari, "Are they going to—to harm Kaiyo's son?"

Ari shook his head. "No, no… this is how we make peace. A child must be given to the enemy village in a solemn ritual."

"Forever?" Don queried.

"Yes. Haenam will raise the boy as their own. He is now the Peace Child. The peace will last as long as he lives."

A Haenam leader returned to the center of the clearing. Holding the baby high over his head, he announced, "Haenam and Kamur… behold, your Peace Child!"

Immediately, the crowds on both sides erupted into joyful cheers, holding hands and jumping in celebration. Don smiled. *Thank you, Lord, for peace in one way at least.*

But as the day wore on, Don couldn't stop replaying the ritual over and over in his mind. Although he and

Carol were overjoyed by the long-prayed-for peace, the weight of Kaiyo's and Wumi's sacrifice hung heavy in Don's mind.

For God so loved the world, that He gave His only Son...

The words of John 3:16 flashed through Don's mind in an instant, and suddenly, it all became clear.

That's it! God's answer to our prayers! That's how we can explain His gospel to them, through the Peace Child!

***

Sunlight poured through the door of the crowded meeting hall, as Sawis sat shoulder to shoulder with every eye watching Don, who stood, Bible in hand.

"You see, just like Kamur and Haenam were enemies, God and all humanity were enemies, because we sinned and hated God. And just like you needed a child to bring peace between your villages, the whole world needed someone to bring peace between God and man. God gave His only Son, Jesus, to be our Peace Child, to die for our sins so that we could have peace with Him again. And although your human Peace Child will eventually die, Jesus died and rose again to live eternally, so that the peace between us and God stands forever."

Don watched the Sawis sit in stunned silence. They could hardly believe that there existed a God so loving that He would give His only Son as a Peace Child for them.

A warrior finally broke the silence, "Tuan Don, tell us more."

***

As the years passed, God opened the eyes and hearts of the Sawis. Don and Carol continued to share the gospel with them—now using the Peace Child as an analogy—and thousands surrendered their lives to Christ, casting aside their traditions of witchcraft, revenge, and cannibalism which had enslaved them for so long.

The Richardsons were overwhelmed with gratitude; there was finally a lasting peace among the Sawis... not just because of an earthly mediator, but because of a Heavenly Peace Child.

Don and Carol developed an alphabet for the Sawis, which Don then used to translate the entire New Testament so that the Sawis could read the truth for themselves in their native tongue.

One evening, Carol and Don stood in their doorway, looking out over the bustling village. Carol smiled at her three sons, Steve, Shannon, and Paul, as they ran past, laughing and playing with the Sawi boys. Looking down at his wife, Don tried to think of words to sum up what he was feeling. All he could say was, "Thank God…"

Carol smiled and leaned against her husband's shoulder. "Amen."

***

Decades later, in 2012…

A small pontoon plane glided gently over the lonely river, getting nearer and nearer to the surface each second. On the shore, hundreds of people stood waiting, wearing headdresses and holding drums, watching the plane descend.

At last, the plane touched down on the water and maneuvered its way over to the crowded dock. The door opened, and joyous cheers exploded from the crowd of Sawis as an elderly white head appeared. Don Richardson stood grinning and waving at the people.

Celebratory singing and chanting broke out, and as Don disembarked he was engulfed in embraces and greetings from old friends. He was followed by his three grown sons, also smiling and waving excitedly to the people.

Fifty years had passed since Don and Carol had first landed on that muddy shore, ready to share the gospel of peace. After 15 years in New Guinea ministering to the Sawis and other tribes, Don and Carol had returned to America to continue exhorting others to reach the nations for Christ.

The Sawis and their home could not be more different since the first time Don and Carol had encountered them.

Don and his sons were given a tour of the village, and they couldn't stop smiling at the transformation they saw; everyone was well-clothed, hundreds of sturdy houses had been built, and joy hung in the air like a pleasant aroma. There were elderly Sawis for the first time in centuries, and Don smiled to see so many healthy children, thanks to the medical practices Carol had taught the women.

At this thought, Don looked down at his wedding ring, his heart aching a little.

Eight years earlier, Carol had succumbed to cancer and gone home to be with her Lord, whom she had served faithfully for so long.

Don looked up and surveyed the thriving village. He thought of Carol and remembered their time with the Sawis with happiness.

He sighed, lost in his thoughts, and stood overwhelmed with joy and gratitude for what he saw: peace.

3

TRANSGENDERED TO TRANSFORMED

LAURA PERRY SMALTS

The six-year-old girl glared up at her mother, arms folded. Francine Perry, exhausted from a long day, groaned and shook her head in frustration.

"I don't understand you, Laura! Don't you ever listen? At church, or school, or at home? Why can't you learn?"

Laura responded, cheeks pink with anger, "You *always* blame me! You never understand…"

At the sound of crunching plastic, both of them turned around to look at Laura's twelve-year-old brother, Brian, standing in the doorway holding the remains of a model airplane.

Francine whirled back to address Laura.

"Look at him, Laura! Brian worked so hard on his airplane, and now you've destroyed it. You should be ashamed of yourself!"

Laura started to speak up again, "But Mommy, I wasn't even—"

"Go to your room, Laura!" Francine said through gritted teeth.

Laura huffed angrily and stormed upstairs. She slammed her bedroom door and threw herself onto the bed. She had no tears to cry, only a furious pressure in her chest that felt like it would crush her from the inside.

Mommy hates me, she doesn't care... she only loves Brian, that's why she says I'm a "daddy's girl," and I'm always getting in trouble... Mommy loves boys more...

Then a new thought entered Laura's mind.

I wish I was a boy...

***

Laura's parents, Paul and Francine Perry, had a steady marriage and were heavily involved in their church. They had three children and seemed to be raising a picture-perfect Christian family... with the exception of their youngest daughter, Laura. She was a naturally mischievous child and, in spite of all of her parents' best efforts at strict discipline and stern lectures, Laura was rebellious and constantly getting into trouble, unlike her mild-mannered brother Brian.

Laura didn't understand that one reason she was always in more trouble was because she was much younger and less mature. Laura craved affection from her mother, but in Laura's mind her mother only saw the need for more correction. When Laura called out for the attention she desperately desired, her mother didn't respond with gentle hugs or "I love you," but rather, with "Stop misbehaving!"

Laura couldn't understand why she was punished while Brian was adored, and gradually, she began wondering, *What if I were a boy?* Eventually, these idle thoughts devolved into secret, full-blown fantasies about actually living as a male.

Then, at eight years of age, Laura was sexually violated by a boy her age.

This experience added a whole new dimension to the confusion and darkness that had taken root in Laura's soul. Too ashamed to tell her parents, she lay in bed at night, feeling dirty and guilty, while simultaneously craving more of what she had experienced.

Laura became increasingly sexualized as she entered high school and began using pornography by the age of 15. She had numerous boyfriends, casually slept around and partied, and even smuggled alcohol into her high school. She felt desperately insecure about her gender and identity and consequently turned to male friends for affirmation. But as each boy she slept with rejected her, Laura began to view her female body as they did: disposable.

Late one night, 16-year-old Laura stumbled into her home after a party, hungover and irritable. She dumped her things on the counter and slowly began making her way up the stairs to her bedroom. The light flipped on, and Laura jumped. It was Laura's mom, Francine, in her pajamas, disheveled and furious.

"Laura, what on earth are you doing? We told you to be back by 10:30… it's almost 2 a.m.! What were you thinking?"

Laura rolled her eyes and slurred, "I dunno—I just lost track of time, I guess."

She tried to head into her room but Francine cut her off with a hand on her arm. Laura spun angrily, shoving her mother's hand away.

Francine's voice was tinged with desperation, "Laura, we've sent you on mission trips, and we've been in counseling with you for over a year… what's it going to take? You can't keep living like this!"

Something snapped inside Laura. Balling her hands into fists, she yelled into Francine's face, "What's it gonna *take*? To do what? Make me perfect like you?!"

Laura clenched her jaw and snarled through gritted teeth, "I will *never* be like you… I hate God, I hate church, I hate you. I don't see the point in being a Christian and *you* can't make me one!"

Laura shoved past her mom, slammed the door to her room and collapsed onto her bed. Tears trickled from her eyes as she imagined what it would be like for her mother to come in, cradle Laura in her arms, and whisper, "I love you."

But no, Laura thought. *She could never love me, because I'm not a boy. She's always just trying to fix me…*

Laura drifted off to sleep, head aching, face still wet with tears, and feeling like she was swimming alone in a black sea of despair.

***

Twenty-one-year-old Laura was attending college to earn a degree in computer science and living in her own small apartment. Laura's quest for affirmation and love hadn't ended, and she was still sleeping around. With each new casual sexual encounter, Laura hoped that this would be the experience where she would finally find true love, but instead, Laura only felt more worthless. Nothing was working.

Slowly the thoughts she had toyed with since childhood began to creep back into her mind.

I'd be happy if only I were a man...

And so, late one night, Laura typed into her computer "Girl becoming a boy" just to see what would come up. It loaded for a moment, then several sites appeared. The word "transgender" jumped out at her, and Laura couldn't believe what was reading.

There are other people out there who feel like me!

She quickly joined an online trans support group, and they explained to her the next steps in her journey. One of the members told Laura enthusiastically, "In six months, no one will even know you were ever a girl. With a new wardrobe, haircut, name change, and a few years of hormones... trust us, you won't even recognize yourself!"

In 2007, aged 25, Laura began living full-time as Jake.

***

"Happy Anniversary, Mom and Dad."

Laura set down a small bouquet of flowers on the restaurant table and awkwardly hugged Paul and Francine. Laura couldn't miss the shock in her mother's eyes, and she knew her mom was taking in the new butch haircut and masculine clothing Laura was sporting.

It had been months since Laura's parents had seen her, and she had only reluctantly accepted their invitation to have dinner with them on their wedding anniversary.

About halfway through the meal, Paul excused himself to go to the restroom. Francine leaned forward, gazing intently at her daughter, and asked softly, "Laura, are you *trying* to look like a man?"

Laura's eyes filled with tears, but she nodded, running a hand through her close-cropped hair.

"Yes, Mom. I am."

Francine's face went white.

Tears pouring down her face, Laura continued roughly, "I—I've been taking hormones... that's why my voice is lower, and—and I'm finally starting to grow facial hair. And I only wear men's clothes now."

Laura clenched her jaw, and her voice broke with emotion and anger.

"I hate girls. I hate that God made me a girl—so I'm changing that. I'm taking control of my own life."

"Laura…"

The silent agony in Francine's eyes nearly broke Laura's heart. But then it hardened again, and Laura said in a low tone, swiping at her tears, "Don't call me Laura anymore, Mom. My name is Jake."

As Laura got into her car later that night, she pulled out her phone and saw her recent calls. She saw the entries for "Dad" and "Mom."

Why do I even need them?

She remembered the disappointed looks on their faces at the restaurant.

I'd be better off without them. They're just holding me back, tied to the past.

Over the next few months, Laura told herself she was wildly happy with her new lifestyle, but there was always a nagging feeling lurking in the back of her mind that the new clothes, new haircut, new voice… none of them had turned her into the person she longed to be, the person who felt valued and loved. She felt she needed something more to solidify her new identity. Something drastic.

***

Monitors beeped softly around the operating table, and Laura stared numbly up at the ceiling.

The day had finally come; Laura was going to have a double mastectomy and chest reconstruction.

Laura looked down at the dotted lines crisscrossing her skin and shuddered at the thought of the surgeon slicing along those lines. This surgery would allow her to be considered male by law, and she believed this was the final step to achieving that ever-elusive happiness.

As she lay waiting for the anesthesiologist, her mind wandered back to a letter she had recently received from Aunt Shirley, a dear friend of Laura's mother.

"Satan has his hold on you, Laura... You're swimming deeper into a darkness that will drown you... We're throwing you a lifeline, please don't push us away... run away from this, and run to Christ!"

Laura had torn up the letter.

But now, lying under the harsh lights, Aunt Shirley's words came back to Laura, particularly those about the eternal punishment promised to those who rejected God. Laura knew from her years of church attendance that salvation from Hell didn't come from following rules, but rather from repenting of sinfulness toward Christ and asking Him for salvation from it.

Laura had chosen to reject all of that. But now, she was having second thoughts.

What if they put me under, and I never wake back up? I know I'll go to Hell...

All of Laura's adrenaline turned into pure terror, and she squeezed her eyes shut, trembling.

God, I don't want to go to Hell... please, don't let me die here! Please, Jesus, let me survive... But I'm not calling off the surgery. I don't want to die, but I don't want to live as a woman either...

Six hours later, Laura opened her eyes. A nearby nurse smiled.

"You're awake, Mr. Perry! Congratulations, the surgery was completely successful... Are you pleased with your results?"

Laura lifted the sheets and glanced down at her bandaged chest. She smiled.

***

Ecstatic after her surgery, Laura completely forgot her desperate prayer. She finally felt like the man she'd always wanted to be.

A few weeks later, Laura's boss, a lesbian named Ellen*, came into Laura's cubicle at work and asked her what was wrong.

"You've been moping around the office, you haven't been working as hard, you're depressed... what happened to the old Jake?"

Laura was stunned. Couldn't Ellen see how happy she was after the surgery? She tried to forget about the conversation, but she couldn't get it out of her mind.

She's right... I'm not actually any happier. The surgery didn't really change who I am... it just changed what I look like. My driver's license says "male," but that doesn't actually change me.

Laura felt a great weight settling over her, but she twitched her shoulders angrily.

No! I am happy! It's just these female hormones... If I get rid of those, I'll get rid of all these emotions. Then I'll really be the man I've always wanted to be.

A few months later, Laura had all her female organs surgically removed. For a few weeks, Laura was thrilled, but when the novelty wore off Laura again found it had done nothing to bring her the peace she craved. Would she ever find an identity that satisfied her?

***

"Laura, I'm not sure if this is still your number, but I was wondering if you would be willing to set up a website for my ladies' Bible study? You know I'm no good with computers… I'd be happy to pay you, just let me know if you're interested. Love, Mom."

Laura jumped on the opportunity as soon as she heard the voicemail. Although it frustrated her that her mom continued to use her old name, Laura needed the money and knew how to create websites.

One late night, while she was up working on the website, it occurred to Laura that it might be a nice touch to add descriptions of all her mom's recorded teachings. Without thinking, she started playing one of the lessons.

Before she realized what was happening, Laura couldn't turn it off.

The way her mom was speaking about this faithful, loving God… it felt foreign, and certainly didn't sound like the mom Laura had known—and despised—all these years. It didn't sound like the God who was so intent on external appearances and perfect behavior.

She wanted to know more. A few days later, she picked up her phone and dialed a number she hadn't called in years.

"Hey Mom… I know we haven't talked on the phone for a long time… but… I had some questions about your website I'm building."

"It's so good to hear your voice, Laura," Francine replied. "What can I answer for you?"

Laura stammered her way through the call for 20 minutes, but eventually got around to the real reason she was calling.

"I—I've been listening to the lessons you've been teaching at your Bible study... you know, just so I can write descriptions for the lessons."

"Oh really? What do you think?"

"It was... really different... I guess I just want to understand a little more. Is that ok?"

"Of course!" Francine beamed.

After Francine thoughtfully answered Laura's questions and they hung up the phone, Laura realized something. She had just held a 30-minute conversation with her mom, and Francine had not corrected or reprimanded her a single time.

Laura kept listening to the Bible studies and inexplicably felt drawn deeper into the Bible with each lesson. That first call to her mom turned into another, and another, until six months later Laura realized she was calling her mom for answers almost daily.

During one of their calls, Laura began lamenting a difficult work situation. After hearing her daughter out, Francine replied simply, "Honey, you're just going to have to trust the Lord."

Laura couldn't believe what she was hearing. Her mom had always had all the answers during Laura's growing-up years and had often spoken to Laura with a tone of condescension, but recently, her mom had seemed so content, so loving, so at peace… so different from the judgmental, critical mother of Laura's youth.

"Mom, what's happened to you?"

Francine chuckled softly. "Well honey, the Lord's been working on me, teaching me some things… I've always thought I had to check all the boxes, for myself and for you kids… but the Lord's been showing me that I can't change hearts, yours or anyone else's. Only He can. And all I need to do is obey Him and follow His plan, instead of trying to make my own."

Long after they had hung up, Laura continued to hear those words over and over. A thought entered her mind.

If God can change Mom, maybe He can do the same for me… I'm already in such a different place than I was six months ago! What's happening to me?

Laura continued to wrestle, drawn in by the Word and her mother's love, but still weighed down by the anger and bitterness from her childhood.

One night, Laura couldn't fight anymore. Shaking with sobs, she got onto her knees in her apartment, and prayed, "Jesus, I am a sinner. I've rebelled against You, I've prayed to Satan, I've hated You… I don't know if You could ever forgive me… but God, will You please save me?"

Immediately, Laura felt a warm peace flood over her, and she realized all of her searching and striving was over. God had won the battle for Laura's heart, and that night her identity was sealed in Christ.

***

I want to be a man of God!

Immediately after becoming a Christian, Laura knew she wanted to live her life to honor her new Savior.

I'm going to be a man who follows the Lord anywhere He leads!

In the days and weeks that followed, Laura zealously sought the Lord, and He began to produce true fruit in her heart. But as she grew closer to the Lord, the Holy Spirit began to convict Laura of her transgender lifestyle. At first, she tried to push the thoughts away.

Jake can be a follower of Jesus just as much as Laura can…

But God wasn't going to leave Laura in the lie of her broken identity, and try as she might, Laura couldn't shake the weight of guilt she felt. One day, on her way to work, she turned on the car radio to listen to her favorite Christian speaker, Dr. Everett Piper.

"Friends, today we are going to tackle a somewhat difficult, but necessary, topic. I would like to speak to all those who are under the bondage of the transgender lifestyle."

Oh no! Not this! thought Laura.

Dr. Piper continued, "I am speaking to those letting their feelings and impulses define their identity. In Galatians 5:17 it says, 'For the desires of the flesh are against the Spirit, and the desires of the Spirit are against the flesh, for these are opposed to each other, to keep you from doing the things you want to do.' And here's the good news in verse 24, friends, 'And those who belong to Christ Jesus have crucified the flesh with its passions and desires.'"

Laura squirmed uncomfortably in her seat. She left the radio on, but mentally tuned out what was being said. *It doesn't matter... he'll have a new topic next week.*

But he didn't. It was the same topic again the next week, and the week after. It was as if the broadcasts had been designed just for her.

At first, Laura stubbornly ignored what the Holy Spirit was speaking to her about God's plan for gender and identity, but as the weeks went by the door to her heart began to slowly crack open. Cautiously, Laura began to listen.

"Listen, friends, you are more than just your feelings. Your emotions don't define who you are. Would you like to know what really defines you?"

What? My circumstances? thought Laura.

"Who God says you are. That's what defines you. That's right. Because in the Garden of Eden, God created the first people. Male and female. Adam and Eve. And God doesn't make mistakes. In fact, He called that garden perfect and His creation perfect."

Laura listened closer.

"And today, you're here listening because God knitted you together in your mother's womb just the way He wanted. And if you're dissatisfied with your body, with your identity, with who you are... you feel that you could never live with the body that God gave you... then I have news for you."

Laura held her breath.

"You are more than your feelings or desires. You are not an animal, enslaved to your instincts. You have a will... and can choose your behavior despite how you feel. And Christ has a greater purpose for you and a far greater calling on your life than just doing whatever makes you happy."

Laura looked away as tears crept into her eyes.

"Stop running. Let God define your identity, and follow Him."

***

A few weeks passed, with Dr. Piper's words still ringing in her ears. One day, Laura called Francine to ask what the latest Bible study had been about.

"Oh, we're studying the judgment seat of Christ. Would you like to hear about it?"

Half an hour later, Laura hung up the phone and dropped her head into shaking hands. She felt pierced with conviction, and terrified.

Jesus, I'm not ready to stand before Your throne... she prayed. *Mom was telling me that some are going to stand there ashamed, having done nothing for You... I know I can't do anything to save myself, but I don't want to waste my life! What would it take for me to hear "Well done, good and faithful servant"?*

She was startled by God's clear yet quiet response: *What name would I call?*

What do you mean, Lord? Laura prayed.

If you stood before Me tonight, what name would I call? Jake... or Laura?

Laura didn't know how to answer.

But then, the Lord whispered, lovingly, and tenderly: *Laura, let Me tell you who you are.*

The truths Laura had recently uncovered began flooding her mind.

If anyone is in Christ, [she] is a new creation (2 Corinthians 5:17)... put on the new self, created after the likeness of God in true righteousness and holiness (Ephesians 4:24)... the Spirit of life has set you free in Christ Jesus from the law of sin and death (Romans 8:2)... [you] are His workmanship, created in Christ Jesus for good works (Ephesians 2:10)...

Laura's eyes filled with tears.

***

It was July 24, 2016. Laura stood in the doorway, taking one last look around her apartment.

It was dim and seemed so bare after Laura had trashed or given away everything from her old life. Laura sniffed and wiped her eyes. Leaving the entire life she had known for the past decade was difficult and frightening. But then she remembered the truth from Colossians 3.

If then you have been raised with Christ, seek the things that are above, where Christ is... For you have died, and your life is hidden with Christ in God.

Yes, this move felt like death, and in a way it was. It was the death of "Jake Perry."

Resolutely Laura turned and picked up her bags, walked out of the apartment, and closed the door firmly behind her. "Jake" was dead, but Laura was more alive than ever, with the breath of the Holy Spirit filling her soul.

***

"I now pronounce you husband and wife! Mr. Smalts, you may kiss your bride."

Laura felt her heart would erupt with joy.

In May 2022, Laura was wed to the man of her dreams, Perry Smalts. As the newlyweds walked down the aisle hand in hand, Laura looked over and caught her new husband's gentle eyes, and her heart thrilled at the undeniable adoration she saw in them. God had truly redeemed her, all of her, and blessed her beyond her wildest imaginings.

Today, Laura and her husband speak on the topic of transgenderism through their ministry, Eden's Redemption, and use their testimonies to share the gospel. Together, they offer resources and hope to those who are struggling with their own gender identity, declaring to others the transforming work God has done in Laura's life.

4

MIRACLE AT THE PENTAGON

BRIAN BIRDWELL

Brian opened his eyes, and with a great effort lifted his head to look around from where he was lying face down on the floor.

What's happening…?

Dark, thick smoke billowed around his face, and he couldn't make out anything around him. There was a roaring noise…

Then, in two seconds, Brian's senses rushed back.

Excruciating pain unlike anything he'd ever experienced racked his entire body. His arms, legs, back, face… everywhere…

Brian coughed as he inhaled choking, black smoke that made his lungs burn.

Darkness was everywhere... but there was an orange glow coming from behind Brian.

Wait, no... the glow is coming from me...

Horror dawned in Brian's mind. His entire body was on fire.

***

Just hours earlier, the morning of September 11, 2001, had begun just like any other Tuesday. Brian had kissed Mel on the cheek, peeked through the bedroom door to catch a glimpse of his 12-year-old son, Matt, fast asleep, then headed out at 5 a.m. for a full day of work at the Pentagon.

Brian stepped off of the bus onto the Pentagon grounds and walked briskly through security and scanned his access badge to enter the inner hallway ramp on his way to his second-floor office.

After serving as a U.S. Army officer for 17 years, Brian had just been promoted to Lieutenant Colonel nine months prior. And while he had avoided a Pentagon assignment for as long as he could, now he was here in Washington, D.C.

Brian was a committed Christian and was convinced of the providence of God at work in all things, including placing him in this particular job at this particular time, and was therefore determined to serve his country to the best of his ability.

Brian traveled down the long corridors to his office, nodding good morning to the colleagues he passed on his way. One of Brian's co-workers, Cheryle, was already typing away at her computer when he arrived, and their other co-worker, Sandy, joined them soon after. As the morning hours dwindled away, the day passed as usual, with only an occasional phone call.

A little before 9 a.m., Sandy's phone rang again, and when she picked up, a smile spread across her face. She covered the mouthpiece and whispered, "It's my daughter, Sam, in New York—"

Sandy put the phone back up to her ear. As she listened, her smile disappeared and was replaced by horror. Eyes wide, she turned to the others, "A plane just crashed into one of the World Trade towers."

As soon as Sandy hung up, they flipped on the TV and watched in silent shock as clouds of smoke billowed from the North Tower. As they flipped from channel to channel, it was the same horrific scene everywhere. Ugly, black smoke rising into the sky.

TV newscasters were lamenting the tragic accident. Brian shook his head slowly. "This wasn't an accident…"

Minutes later, Brian was proven correct. He and the women watched on live television as another plane soared through the sky and crashed into the second tower, creating a massive fireball. They could hardly believe what they were seeing was reality. As chaos broke loose in New York City, Brian, Cheryle, and Sandy knelt on the office floor.

Brian led a simple prayer, asking God to protect the police officers, firefighters, and other first responders and all of those in danger because He was going to do the bulk of the life-saving that day.

For the next several minutes, Brian and his co-workers huddled around the TV, each lost in thought, trying to comprehend the suffering that those in the Twin Towers were going through at that very moment.

Brian eventually stood up. "I'm going to the restroom, be right back."

The women nodded, eyes glued to the television.

A few minutes later, Brian came out of the restroom and began walking back toward his office.

Then, the world exploded.

***

Brian was on fire.

The pain was unbearable, and in all of his Army training, nothing had prepared Brian for something like this. He was engulfed in darkness, illuminated only by the flames licking away at his body.

All around him, alarms shrieked and straining metal groaned. The chaos of building materials was everywhere. Poisonous fumes that reminded him of jet fuel flooded down Brian's throat and set his lungs ablaze, choking him.

Brian's mind was reeling. *I have to stand up... I have to get out of here...*

He struggled to rise, but his knees collapsed.

Again, Brian tried to stand, tried to feel, tried to find the wall, a door—anything to help him get up.

There's nothing here... I can't see...

The thick black smoke enveloped him, clouding his vision and making it impossible to think.

Angry flames consumed Brian's body, melting his clothes and flesh. Brian tried desperately to get to his feet once again, only to collapse a second time. Finally, after multiple failed attempts, he remained crumpled on the floor, unable to endure the pain another moment.

Then, Brian did the one thing the Army had drilled into him since day one never to do: He surrendered.

Brian cried out into the chaos, "Jesus, I'm coming to see You!"

His eyes swelling shut with agonizing burns, Brian waited in torment for death to come.

For a brief moment, the pain vanished and time slowed. Brian thought about Mel and Matt that morning and wished with all his heart that he could have truly said goodbye. He would have held Mel longer, woken up Matt and hugged him, told them both how much they meant to him. If only he had known that this would be his last day with them on earth…

The next time I see them… will be in eternity.

Brian closed his eyes and lay in the excruciating flames waiting to meet Jesus face to face, to see the gates of Heaven open wide, to hear, "Well done, My good and faithful servant."

He wondered what it would feel like when his soul left his body.

Will I fall unconscious before I die?

But still, he waited. And waited.

Then, Brian felt something cold and wet trickle down his cheek.

Water... how?

He opened his eyes again and comprehended the first miracle.

Of all the places he could have been blown, of all the areas he could have fallen, by God's providence, he had landed directly beneath one of the last remaining functioning fire sprinklers, which was now dousing his flaming body.

The cool water gave him fresh clarity and hope. God had kept him alive, at least for now.

I have to get out of here, while I still have a chance.

Using every ounce of his strength to raise his head an inch, Brian finally spotted in the distance a glimmer of light far down the corridor—the hallway out of the blaze and smoke.

Safety.

If I can just get that far...

With a renewed sense of purpose, Brian used the wall he had collapsed beside to pull himself up and painstakingly began shuffling away from the blast zone, bracing his charred hands and sliding his feet. Each step was agonizing, and after what seemed like an eternity, Brian began approaching the end of the corridor... but where he should have been able to see the escalators, he saw nothing but a solid wall.

The automatic fire containment doors in the Pentagon had closed, locking Brian in with the raging inferno behind him.

Did I survive earlier, only to die now?

But then, God brought about the second miracle of the day.

At that moment, a locked door swung open, and a man stepped out, spotting Brian through the black haze, and calling behind him for additional help.

Brian took one more step before collapsing to the floor a final time as more men came rushing through the door.

He recognized one of the men, Bill McKinnon, a fellow officer and a good friend. Brian heard Bill shout, "Guys, over here! We've got someone from the impact zone!"

Am I so badly burned that Bill doesn't recognize me?

The men ran through the blistering heat, then bent over Brian's seared body, rolling him over. Then they gripped his arms to lift him.

Bill glanced at everyone, "We've gotta get out of here… on the count of three, lift!"

"STOP! STOP, LET GO!" Brian screamed, as chunks of flesh fell from his arms and body like dried wax. The men tried repositioning Brian but to the same effect. Brian's burned flesh was like putty and peeled off his blistered frame with even the slightest contact.

Finally, the men gripped each other's hands and slid their arms carefully beneath Brian, taking flesh with them, then lifted him and rushed away.

***

Hundreds of confused and terrified people flooded the Pentagon's halls, running to the nearest exits. The men wove through the crowd cradling Brian, and Bill yelled over the hubbub, "They think a plane flew into the side of the building! Probably the same people who hit the World Trade Center, but they don't know for sure…"

The group finally burst into the innermost area of the Pentagon. Bill and the other men laid Brian down in a makeshift medical triage area.

"They'll take care of you here!" the men shouted, as they rushed off to search for more casualties.

As survivors continued running past, Dr. John Baxter, an Air Force Colonel and flight surgeon, surveyed Brian's burned body, which was charred to a crisp and oozing blood. He was unrecognizable.

Dr. Baxter began looking for any area of Brian's body where he could still insert an IV, then quickly removed Brian's leather shoes. The shoes had mostly protected Brian's feet, so the doctor put a morphine shot in Brian's right foot and an IV in his left, the only places he could see any veins.

Brian began to cough and shake uncontrollably. All of the aerosolized jet fuel and black smoke he had inhaled was now causing his lungs to blister and pool fluid. Brian felt like he was on fire and drowning at the same time.

Through his swollen eyes, Brian saw a woman stop beside him and kneel, a Bible in her hands.

"Sir, my name is Natalie. I'm a Christian. I was evacuating, but I saw you and I felt prompted by God to come pray with you. Would you like to say the Lord's Prayer with me?"

"Y—y—yes..."

Natalie opened her Bible. Together, as Brian struggled to breathe and speak, they recited the passage from Matthew 6:9–14:

"Our Father in heaven,
hallowed be your name.
Your kingdom come,
your will be done,
*   on earth as it is in heaven.*
Give us this day our daily bread,
and forgive us our debts,
*   as we also have forgiven our debtors.*
And lead us not into temptation,
*   but deliver us from evil."*

As Brian's body continued to spasm violently, Natalie read Psalm 23 over him. "Even though I walk through the valley of the shadow of death, I will fear no evil, for you are with me..."

The poignant words gripped Brian's heart, and his lips moved soundlessly along with Natalie as she read.

Moments later, Brian was placed on a body board and then lifted onto a small vehicle that rushed him out to the equally chaotic parking lot, where he was loaded into a Ford Expedition. A nurse hopped into the back and yelled at the driver, "He's critical! Drive him to Georgetown Hospital—it's the only one I know how to get to!"

On a day that seemed to define chaos, God was in total control, orchestrating a third remarkable miracle. Georgetown University Hospital would have usually been deemed smaller and less equipped to handle serious emergencies like Brian's, but on this day, one of the top three burn-and-trauma specialty doctors in the entire Washington, D.C., metropolis, Dr. Michael Williams, was providentially on duty.

Because all United States airspace had been shut down by the terrorist attacks, there were no medical evacuation helicopters transporting patients between hospitals, so Brian was the hospital's only patient and received the entire emergency room's undivided attention.

***

Beep... Beep... Beep...

Several grim-faced nurses attended to the countless life support systems surrounding Brian. Apart from the monitors and sensors, the only other noise was Brian's labored breathing.

Dr. Williams stepped around an IV stand and walked up to the side of Brian's hospital bed. Even through his swollen eyes, Brian could see in Dr. Williams' countenance just how grave the situation was. Brian was plastered in scorched blood and had charred flesh dangling from him; he had been burned on 60% of his body, and 40% of those burns were third-degree. Brian understood his life hung in the balance.

"Colonel Birdwell, we're going to do the best we possibly can for you. We're going to sedate and then intubate you. Is there anything else you'd like to say before you go under?"

I'm so badly burned… my body will swell… they're going to have to cut off my wedding ring before it turns into a tourniquet…

Brian, struggling to speak, rasped hoarsely, "T—take m—my wedding ring…"

If I can't say goodbye in person, at least Mel and Matt will know I thought of them until the end. Lord, if I don't wake… then please be with them. Be a Father to Matt and a Provider to Mel.

The nurse nodded soberly and began to carefully ease Brian's ring off his finger. But even pulling it as tenderly as she could, the flesh on Brian's charred finger couldn't bear the resistance of the gold ring, and peeled away, exposing the damaged tissue beneath… yet Brian felt nothing.

Only peace.

God gave me the job at the Pentagon in the first place, and purposefully put me at work this morning. He caused me to be out of my office at the exact moment the explosion occurred, and designed for the functioning sprinklers to be directly over my flaming body. And then He sent men to rescue me. I don't know what God's next plan for me is, but I know I can trust Him.

Turning to the doctor, Brian feebly said, "G—give my ring to my wife. T—t—tell her—I love her."

Tears leaked from Brian's eyes, not from pain, but from gratitude that God had given him this opportunity to say goodbye to his wife and son through the symbolism of preserving his ring. And for the second time that day, he surrendered himself to his Savior.

Jesus, I'm ready…

The hospital chaplain came up beside the bed and began to pray over Brian, while the medical staff focused on the impending operation ahead.

"Lord, we know You have brought Brian here for a reason, and that You have placed Dr. Williams and the rest of our team here for a reason. You are not only the Great Physician, but also the highest in our chain of command. If it is Your will for Brian to live, we will salute that flag and move forward with that mission of survival. But if You're calling him home to be with You today, we'll submit to Your plans and salute that flag too. Your will be done, Lord. In Christ's name, Amen."

Brian painfully cracked open his eyes and made eye contact with Dr. Williams. "L—let's get on w—with it."

Brian closed his eyes while the nurses placed an oxygen mask over his face and began administering general anesthesia. As Brian's head was leaned backward for intubation, he knew he had several excruciating hours of procedures ahead of him, but he felt at total peace.

Your will be done, Lord.

Brian was prepared to say goodbye to his precious family and meet his Lord and Savior on September 11, 2001.

But God had other plans.

***

Despite his critical condition, and near-impossible chance of survival that day, Brian's life was spared. Through a series of countless miracles in the operating room and a long season of recovery, Brian has defied all medical expectations. Over the next four years, Brian underwent 39 procedures and reconstructive surgeries. He suffered through innumerable physical therapy sessions, as he regained the use of his limbs. His skin was grafted with combinations of his own skin, pig skin, and cadaver skin, and through all of Brian's recovery years, Mel has remained by his side, living out her wedding vows faithfully.

The plane that crashed into the Pentagon as part of the 9/11 terrorist attacks killed all 59 passengers and crew on board and killed another 125 people in the Pentagon, including both of Brian's co-workers. The nose of the aircraft slammed into the building at 530 miles per hour, right into the hallway between Brian's office and the restrooms, where he had walked only moments before. Brian had been standing only 15 yards away from the impact of the plane, yet the Lord preserved his life. Brian is the sole survivor from the outer ring of the crash site.

Today, Brian and Mel have been married for over 35 years and live in Texas, where Brian serves as a State Senator.

Brian believes he lives for a purpose: to share his story. The Lord miraculously spared his life and pulled him from the flames of the Pentagon, but more importantly, saved him from an eternal lake of fire by redeeming him through the blood of Jesus Christ. Brian lives as a testimony of the sovereignty of God.

5

ABORTION CLINIC OWNER REBORN

CAROL EVERETT

February, 1973…

"We're ready for you now, miss," the nurse called from the doorway.

There's no other choice…

Carol walked shakily into the operating room, her heartbeat quickening at the sight of the operating table, blinking monitors, and gleaming instruments. As the nurse began to drape her legs, Carol felt cold and numb. The door opened and a doctor came in, tugging off a pair of surgical gloves. Carol noticed they were blotched with red.

"Ready for your abortion?"

She nodded, and the doctor began pulling on another pair of gloves.

***

Harsh lights... stained ceiling... cold slippery plastic...

Carol felt like her lungs were being squeezed. The nightmare of the last few minutes replayed in her mind like a horror movie.

A needle... gleaming instruments... everything going black... waking up in pain... so much blood...

The blurry memories faded, replaced by one burning thought: *I killed my baby.*

The doctor stood at the counter, running a red-splotched washcloth over his instruments. He turned to leave, saying over his shoulder, "All over... you've got your life back."

By taking my baby's...

The nurse began hurriedly stripping away Carol's drapings, glancing at the clock on the wall.

"All right, let's get you up and on your way! Start getting your things together, we've got more ladies coming in..."

Carol lay trembling on the table. *How has my life come to this?*

Memories flashed through her mind. The terror she had felt when, as a 16-year-old, she realized she was pregnant with Jim Bob's baby. The rushed marriage that followed. The divorce. Meeting Tom and feeling her life might finally take a turn for the better. The elation when

Tom had asked her to marry him... and then the promise. The promise that now haunted her.

"Carol, if we're going to marry, you have to promise one thing. If you get pregnant again, you will have an abortion."

Hot tears leaked from Carol's eyes as her answer echoed in the back of her mind. *"OK, Tom, I will."*

Sadness turned to anger as Carol remembered the fateful phone call with her personal doctor, Dr. Johnson.

"You know, Carol, I'm an OB-GYN, but I'm also an abortionist. And although abortion is technically illegal in Texas, I quietly operate in multiple clinics, and if you want I could make this happen for you. And it could be... shall we say, off the books."

She had been desperately reaching out for someone, anyone, to advise her against an abortion. Instead, she had been offered an illegal abortion by a medical professional.

"Ma'am, let's get you on your way!"

Carol was jerked into the present, as the nurse firmly pulled her up from the operating table and hurried her out, beckoning to another woman to come in.

When she arrived at home that evening, Carol longed for tender words and some shred of comfort from Tom. Instead, he sat glued to the TV while she eased herself onto the couch next to him.

"I had the procedure done today." Carol was choking back tears.

Tom hardly glanced at her and said absently, "Well, glad that's over with. It's for the best, you know."

A light rain began to fall as, back at the clinic, a nurse dropped a very small container marked ♀ into the alley dumpster.

***

After her abortion, Carol found herself burdened by an incredible guilt and sadness she could never escape. She turned to alcohol and partying, but nothing brought relief, and Carol instead found her life spiraling into even darker places. Carol's marriage to Tom began to crumble, and she eventually had multiple affairs. At just 30 years old Carol found herself divorced for a second time, with no hope of a happy family in her future, and carrying the heavy weight of having murdered her own child.

Deep down, Carol knew that was what she had done, but she couldn't handle the reality of it. Instead, she rehearsed over and over the justifications she had heard, until they became automatic responses to silence the doubts in her heart.

It's the best choice... You have to choose what's best for the mother... The U.S. Supreme Court just ruled that abortion is legal... It's not a baby, just a glob of tissue... It can't feel anything anyway...

As time went by, Carol managed to ignore most of the guilt by throwing herself relentlessly into her medical supply job, quickly climbing the ladder in the company. As long as she stayed busy enough, the awful thoughts and memories stayed away.

One day, her boss, Chuck, pulled her aside. "Hey Carol, I know that you're looking for some extra money. Well, I own an abortion clinic... would you help me out by just mentioning it to all the doctors you're talking to? I'll give you 25 bucks for every abortion you refer."

Carol hesitated, then shrugged and nodded. *Anything to keep me going... And anyway, abortion really is the best option for a lot of mothers...*

And so, every time a doctor mentioned a complicated or high-risk pregnancy, or a patient looking for abortion options, Carol mentioned Chuck's clinic. After several months, Carol was very pleased with the money she was making on the side.

Early one morning, her phone rang, and when she picked up, she heard Chuck's stressed voice on the line.

"Carol! Thank goodness you picked up—our director for the clinic called in sick, and we have no one to run it today! I know you have great administrative abilities and experience working with medical offices—would you be willing to do it? You'd be doing me a big favor."

Carol hesitated. She thought of the $25 per abortion that she was making. *I want to make sure to maintain a good relationship with Chuck...*

"Umm... sure. I'll be there."

After the first day working in Chuck's clinic, Carol never went back to her old job; somehow, it provided a twisted way to justify her own sin.

Everyone here seems to think having an abortion is ok... mine must have been ok too... I'm actually helping all of these women...

Soon, she found herself repeating over and over, "What's good for the woman..." until her calloused heart could justify its way out of even the most tragic situations.

Late-term abortion. *What's good for the woman...*

A woman who didn't want to "ruin her perfect body." *What's good for the woman...*

Perfectly healthy baby who was simply unwanted. *What's good for the woman...*

She soon recruited Dr. Harvey Johnson—her OB-GYN and the doctor who had also performed her abortion—to become the head abortionist at Chuck's clinic. After a few months, Carol realized that this profession could be more to her than just a coping mechanism. As she looked at the financial records for the clinic and saw the profits that the clinic was bringing in, a plan began to unfold in Carol's mind.

***

"OK, let's get down to business; for our end-of-year recap, I put together a couple of stats for us to look over..."

Carol glanced up from her papers to see Harvey rolling his eyes at his live-in girlfriend, Fredi, sitting beside him.

Glaring at him, Carol continued, "OK, to review the timeline... Harvey and I left Chuck's clinic at the beginning of this year to start our own clinic. You—" Carol pointed the pen at Fredi, "—wanted in on it, so we started working together. In the first month we performed 45 abortions—"

"Well, I did," Harvey interjected, "you two just helped out with the easy stuff."

Carol shot him another icy glare, "—and this month, we did 545. Not bad, but we can do better."

She slid a map towards Harvey and Fredi, with five locations in the Dallas area circled.

"I don't know about you two, but I'm planning to be a millionaire by the end of next year. With my current salary of $25 per abortion, that means we would need to perform 40,000 next year. And we can only do that with more clinics."

Harvey and Fredi were nodding, looking over the plans.

"And," Carol added, "we could advertise all over the country that we're the only clinics in the nation offering same-day, late-term abortions..."

Harvey slid the map back. "I like it."

***

One evening a few weeks later, Harvey stuck his head into Carol's office at the clinic, beckoning for her to follow. He explained in a low tone as he led her down the hallway, "We completed this girl's abortion an hour ago, but she tore and hemorrhaged badly..."

Harvey opened the door, and Carol glimpsed a woman on the table, writhing in pain. He continued, "I have a date tonight, so just watch her, and send her home as soon as possible. And make sure the staff keeps their mouths shut."

Carol started to protest, but Harvey rushed off down the hall. Groaning in frustration, Carol entered the operating room.

A new attendant, Darla*, stood looking wide-eyed at all the blood. She asked anxiously, "Is she going to be ok? Maybe this wasn't the right decision for her... should we send her to the hospital down the road?"

Carol interrupted sharply, "No! They don't know us and there would be reporters and questions and inquiries and it's..."

Carol was just about to reprimand Darla with her usual response, "What's best for the woman," but watching the woman's anguished face as she thrashed on the table, Carol remained silent.

Their patient's bleeding finally slowed around 10:30 p.m., enough that Carol decided she was fine to be sent home. As she was leaving, Carol strictly charged her, "If anything happens, call me or Dr. Johnson. If you absolutely have to call a hospital, *only* call this one."

Carol handed her the number for a doctor across town. He knew the clinic, and had enough influence at his hospital to get post-abortive women cared for without questions asked.

The next morning, Carol called Harvey into her office to go over the schedule. Pouring her coffee, she asked absently, "Have you heard anything from that woman yesterday, with the hemorrhaging?"

Harvey's face turned serious. "Didn't you hear? She died last night."

Carol stopped pouring. "What?"

"Yeah, her boyfriend called me at three in the morning, and said she had bad cramps, so I told her to get in a tub of hot water. Her boyfriend called me again later and said she was unconscious and they were headed to the hospital."

"But hot water would pull any blood she had left out of her! Why would you tell her to do that?"

Harvey retorted, "Look, you're not a doctor. I'm the medical professional. What's important is that we've got someone covering for us at the hospital, so I'm not getting any flack for it... and neither are you."

"OK... I'm assuming we'll be closed today?"

"No, we have a packed schedule today. We can't afford to take the day off." Harvey glanced down at his watch. "I have to go, I have an appointment starting in five minutes. See you in a bit."

Carol turned away, a heavy weight settling on her shoulders. She looked at her coffee for a moment, then poured it down the sink. As she walked upstairs, she began repeating fiercely, "What's good for the wom—"

But she cut her familiar mantra short.

***

Several months passed, and Carol managed to push the incident to the back of her mind. Walking into the clinic one morning, she found Harvey and Fredi scrambling around, prepping the consultation room for the next patient. Carol's eyes fell on the ultrasound photos lying on the desk.

"Fredi, how many times do I have to remind you to make sure that the name on the paperwork matches with the name on the ultrasound picture?" Carol snapped. "This isn't the correct ultrasound for the girl you're about to bring back." Carol shot an icy glare in Fredi's direction.

"Oh it doesn't matter which ultrasound picture we use for this consultation," Harvey cut in. "This girl isn't pregnant anyway. We'll just make sure the name is covered up when we show it to her."

"I don't know…" Carol started to say, but Fredi interrupted her with a groan. "Come on, Carol, you're the one always talking about being a millionaire! We already spent time doing the pregnancy test and the ultrasound, we can't afford for her not to pay for an abortion too!"

Harvey spoke up, "Relax, Carol, we do this all the time, and nothing bad has ever come of it. I'm just going to do what I normally do in these scenarios—take the girls into the operating room, poke around a little, then say their abortion is complete. They'll never have a clue."

"*They?*" Carol repeated. "How many girls are you talking about?" The experience with the hemorrhaging woman had made her even more reluctant to take risks that might endanger the clinic.

Fredi pulled Carol to the waiting room door and pointed through the small glass window.

"Right there!"

Carol yanked her arm from Fredi's grasp, and looked out. Three women sat waiting together; two had blonde hair, and the other had long auburn hair, tears streaming from her green eyes.

"Come on, Carol," Fredi said, exasperated. "Let's get on with it. We have a full schedule today!"

"Oh shut up," Carol snapped back. "Fine, let's do it. Who cares... if they want to give us their money, that's up to them."

A few minutes later, Fredi escorted the tearful redhead into the consultation room. Carol stepped forward, gesturing to the table while Harvey smiled and pulled out the grainy sonogram images.

"Please, make yourself comfortable, Ms. Ames.* As you can see, your thoughts were correct; you are clearly pregnant. But fortunately, we can help you with that today..."

***

Holding the phone to her ear, Carol asked absently, "So, who is this guy?"

The CPA on the other end sighed. "Jack Shaw... He's willing to mediate between you, Harvey, and Fredi. All of this fighting between the three of you is going to start cutting into your profit line! You have to find a way to get along... I think you should give Jack a try."

Harvey adamantly refused, but Carol agreed, hardly thinking twice about it; after all, she was going to be a millionaire next year.

And so, a week later, she was sitting down to coffee with Jack, a cheerful man with gentle blue eyes.

By their third meeting, Carol could see that Jack was unlike any other man she'd met. She blurted out, "Why are you so different? I've never met anyone like you! You don't cuss, you don't drink, I bet your wife never wonders where you are at night…"

Jack smiled. "Well, that's the way it works when you have the Lord."

Carol snorted, "I'm a Christian too! I attend church, I keep a Bible in my office, and I pray… I even tithe on all of the money I make!"

Jack asked gently, "Carol, do you believe those things make you a Christian?"

Carol hesitated. Jack leaned forward, looking into her eyes. "Carol, there's something I believe God wants me to tell you. You don't know this, but I'm a pastor. My wife and I have been praying for you and your clinics for a long time. We think there's someone working there that God wants out, and she'll be leaving in 30 days."

"Well, if you're talking about Fredi, I'd be happy for God to make her leave…"

Then Jack's countenance became sober and he spoke passionately, "Carol, right now you are dead in your sins; we all are before we come to Christ. But God loves you so much that He sent His Son, Jesus, to pay for your sins by dying on a cross, so that you can have life with Him forever. You can't be good enough, Carol, can't attend church enough, pray enough, can't do anything to make your dead soul alive. God says that you need only to ask Him, and He will give you life! Would you like to do that right now?"

I pray this prayer and this guy shuts up? Sounds like a good deal.

Carol shrugged and nodded. Jack bent his head, closing his eyes, and Carol did the same, repeating after him, "Lord Jesus, I am a sinner. I ask to be cleansed by Your blood..."

***

The next day, Carol went to work at the clinic as usual, but for some reason she couldn't get Jack's words out of her mind: *There's someone working there that God wants out, and she'll be leaving in 30 days...*

Carol shrugged. "How could Jack know what's about to happen? And why would God care about what happens to my clinic anyway?"

Although she had dismissed the prayer she had mumbled yesterday with Jack, Carol couldn't shake the strange feeling. She sat down at her desk to start on the morning's paperwork. As she pulled out the drawer to grab a folder, her eyes caught on the dusty Bible pushed to the back corner.

Of course I'm a Christian. I have a Bible right here in my clinic! Why do I feel so jumpy? I just need to get the day started and then I'll feel better.

Carol walked into the crowded waiting room to call the first patient. But she froze as she looked around at the women seated there. Her usual enthusiasm was absent, and instead of seeing opportunities to make money, all she could see was the hopelessness in the eyes of the women.

Some were tear-filled, some vacant, some hardened, but all hopeless.

I have to snap out of this...

Carol walked the 15-year-old girl back to her office for a consultation. Sitting down, Carol smiled at her and picked up a folder. "All right, Ms. Williams*, I just have a few forms for you to sign... do you have any questions before I take you back to Dr. Johnson?"

The girl twisted her hands in her lap.

"Will... will it hurt?"

Laughing lightly, Carol said, "Oh no! At most, you might experience mild cramping."

The girl sat in silence for a moment. "Is it—a real baby?"

Carol shook her head emphatically and quoted the lines which, after years of practice, now came readily. "No... it's only tissue. It's up to you if you want to keep it in there; your body, your choice."

Suddenly, the girl stood, and said, her voice quavering, "I—I can't do this..."

The girl quickly left the room, leaving a disgruntled Carol behind her. In frustration, Carol crumpled the papers and threw them in the trash.

Another $25 down the drain...

By the end of that day, several more women had decided against their abortions, and Carol's drive to sell abortions just wasn't there. She had woken up that morning planning to go about the day as usual, but now... it didn't feel right. Finally, Carol got down on her knees in her office.

God, I don't know why You're doing this to me. But I'm not about to throw away my life's work just because You're nagging at me. Just—do something big... show me You mean business.

***

It was Saturday morning, and Carol sat relaxing on the couch, sipping her coffee, with the TV on. It had been a couple of weeks since her conversation with Jack, and Carol was still unsure what to think about what Jack had told her about the clinic... or what he had told her about God.

Carol's phone rang; it was Harvey.

"Have you seen the news?"

"No... why?"

"Turn on CBS now... you need to see this."

Carol quickly hung up and turned to the CBS channel—she almost spat out her coffee. There, holding microphones, stood three female reporters: two blonde and one redhead, with striking green eyes. The newscaster was saying, "—dedicated reporters, willing to do anything for the truth. These women went undercover into this abortion clinic—"

Carol watched in horror as a picture of her clinic came on screen. "They asked for abortions. Before going undercover, it was verified that all three were not pregnant. However... Ms. Ames, will you tell us what happened?"

"Certainly," the redheaded reporter said. "After receiving several tips that this abortion clinic has been performing 'abortions' on women who weren't even pregnant, we had to find out for ourselves. We were all offered abortions despite the fact that not one of us was actually pregnant! We turned down the abortions, and walked out of the clinic without life-altering side effects, but not all women are so fortunate..."

Her words faded away, and Carol sat back in shock.

Well, God... I asked You to show me You mean business. You really don't mess around.

On July 27, 1983, exactly 30 days after her mediation meeting with Jack, Carol packed up her things and left the clinic.

On that day, Carol's career in death was over and God was gently leading her toward the path of life.

***

Over the next year, Carol began attending Jack's church and meeting regularly with him and his wife, Gwen. The once-dusty Bible which had been sitting neglected in the desk drawer at Carol's office was finally opened as Carol searched desperately for answers.

One morning, as Carol was making her way through the book of Psalms, she flipped open to Psalm 139:

"For you formed my inward parts;
  you knitted me together in my mother's womb.
I praise you, for I am fearfully and wonderfully made.
Wonderful are your works;
  my soul knows it very well.
My frame was not hidden from you,

> *when I was being made in secret,*
> *intricately woven in the depths of the earth.*
> *Your eyes saw my unformed substance..."*

Carol was horrified as she reread the words. Words that now felt incriminating.

God fashions all babies' inward parts together... and I've been making money for years by ripping those pieces apart.

Memory after memory raced through her mind.

Tiny hands, feet, and faces... mothers writhing in pain... blood, so much blood...

God was the Author of life, yet for years, Carol had been dealing in death. She had seen babies' unformed substances on sonograms, and confirmed that there was tissue to be eradicated. She had watched Harvey fish around with his instruments as little babies, unable to hide their fragile frames, tried to escape. She had helped reassemble tiny bodies, making sure everything was accounted for.

She had valued unborn babies at $25, and the numbers Carol had once counted up so gleefully now chilled her to the bone.

Thirty-five thousand abortions.

Thirty-five thousand babies dead—and it was her doing.

Carol dropped her head into her hands, condemnation suffocating her soul and spilling over into uncontrollable weeping.

Later that day, Carol found herself at Jack and Gwen's kitchen table pouring out what had happened and finishing with a broken sob, "If it weren't for me, so many children would still be alive today... How can I ever live with myself? How can God ever forgive me?"

Gwen gently took Carol's hand. "Carol, God promises 'There is therefore now no condemnation for those who are in Christ Jesus.'" Carol looked down at the Bible Gwen was holding open at Romans 8 and followed along as Gwen continued. "'For the law of the Spirit of life has set you free in Christ Jesus from the law of sin and death.'"

Gwen looked deep into Carol's eyes. "God promises to never hold your sin over you, Carol. Jesus died to give you life, and not just eternal life in Heaven with Him, but a life free from guilt and shame here on earth."

Jack leaned forward, Bible in hand, and read from Ephesians 2, "'You were dead in the trespasses and sins in which you once walked.'—That was you, Carol. You were dead in your sins, killing babies."

Carol nodded, tears slipping down her cheeks, as Jack began to read again, this time his voice infused with hope.

"'But God, being rich in mercy, because of the great love with which he loved us, even when we were dead in our trespasses, made us alive together with Christ.'"

When we were dead... made us alive... The words echoed in Carol's mind. They seemed too good to be true.

Carol sobbed, "But how could God give life to a woman like me who's been responsible for the deaths of thousands of babies?"

Jack smiled, "It's because God is merciful, like the verse I just read. He doesn't give us the punishment we deserve.

He's forgiven all of us of the terrible things we've done. Even you, Carol."

Carol slowly lifted her downcast eyes. "Even me?"

***

The young woman laughed happily, pointing at the delicate little face on the sonogram.

"Oh my word, she's so cute!"

The woman shook her head in disbelief, her eyes never leaving her little daughter's face.

"I would never have been able to afford this kind of care. If it hadn't been for that first ultrasound here six months ago, I probably would have had an abortion. I can't even imagine that now..."

Carol had sat in rapt attention next to the sonographer who was moving the sensor around for another angle. Finally, Carol spoke up. "That's exactly why I started these crisis pregnancy centers—I wanted to provide prenatal care for low-income women and give them somewhere to go other than straight to an abortion clinic."

The young woman smiled, her gaze turning from Carol back to the screen, then back to Carol again. "Why do you call your center 'The Heidi Group'?"

Carol felt a gentle pang in her heart. She spoke softly, "I had an abortion, a long time ago. Years later I named my little girl Heidi, which means 'hidden.' Even though my baby was hidden from the world, she's still alive in my heart and she inspired me to help other women."

Carol blinked back tears of joy and gratitude as a prayer filled her heart. *Lord, You transformed me from a woman who killed babies to an advocate for unborn lives and the mothers who carry them. You gave me life, and You're using me to give life to the helpless. Truly You are merciful... even to someone like me.*

Carol's heart swelled with joy, and she smiled with the young mother at the baby's face.

6

CHURCH BOY

TROY GAUSE

As the prayer meeting finished, the congregation stood, and the gentle notes of a familiar hymn rose to the church ceiling.

"Amazing grace, how sweet the sound,
That saved a wretch like me.
I once was lost, but now am found,
Was blind but now I see."

In the back row, 19-year-old Troy Gause smiled and hummed along, fingering the small package in his pocket. Sitting there in the pew brought back fond memories of attending the church next door to his house as a young boy. It was there that he had walked down the aisle and professed faith in Jesus. Since then, Troy loved the idea of God and church, along with the sentimental feelings they gave him.

When the hymn ended, he stood up and walked out of the church into the dark streets of New Orleans, Louisiana. His golden chain necklaces glittered in the lamplight, and he kept his hand in his pocket, on the packet of cocaine he had scored before wandering into the prayer meeting. He began to make his usual rounds on the streets, divvying out drugs, while filling his pockets with cash.

And while Troy, an infamous drug dealer in New Orleans known as "Church Boy," used God and religion as a brand—a unique trademark—he ignored the fact that the God he so often referenced might have something to say about the way he was living.

***

Two years later, Troy stood in his mom's kitchen, glaring at her angrily.

"I don't understand why you gotta be so upset! I may be a drug dealer, but I never do drugs myself! And I don't even drink… what do you want me to do? People gotta make a living…"

Jessie's face was streaked with tears.

"That don't mean how you living is right…"

Troy cut her off, retorting, "Don't tell me what to do. I'm in charge of my life now!"

Jessie stared up at her son in silence, then spoke soberly. "No son, you're wrong. You think you're the boss, but you're not in charge. God is the one in charge of you."

Troy watched as tears rolled down his mom's cheeks and her head bent low. In a sorrowful whisper, she said, "I never thought you would turn out this way…"

Troy felt like a knife had been plunged into his heart. Without a word, he turned and walked out the front door.

***

Carrying a heavy duffel bag, Troy walked into the abandoned, run-down casino. A muscular man with earrings and tattooed arms approached, clapping Troy on the shoulder.

"Finally decided to show?"

Troy grinned and punched the man's shoulder.

"Whatcha talking about, Damion*? You're my number one runner, I ain't gonna leave you hanging."

Men who were sprawled around the smoky room quieted down and nodded to Troy, as he walked to the usual corner and dropped his duffel bag onto a table.

"Let's get to it…"

Troy unzipped the bag, and began to pull out packages of various drugs, as the men piled their cash payments beside him. They stashed the majority of the packages for resale on the streets, and they pocketed some for personal use.

After the transactions were made, the alcohol was brought out; the men got more drunk as the night went on. Troy didn't drink, but he was right in the middle of the rowdy gang.

At one point, Troy said, thumbing through his stack of cash, "You know what, fellas? One day, we're all gonna be in Heaven…"

The group laughed raucously, as Damion slurred, "Church Boy be preaching again, y'all!"

Troy grinned, as his pile of bills continued to grow.

***

"Troy, listen… I can't tell you who, but somebody just called and told me that bad people out there are gonna set you up, and hurt you bad… Please, whatever you do, don't go nowhere with nobody, you're not safe!"

Clenching his jaw, Troy felt anger building inside, listening to his mom's anxious voice over the phone.

"Mom, don't you know who I am? Ain't nobody gonna touch me! I'm one of the most well-known drug dealers in New Orleans: *they're* all scared of *me!* Don't call me about this again."

Troy slammed the phone down.

A few minutes later, it rang again. Frustrated, Troy snatched it up, but was surprised to hear the voice of his friend's dad, Anthony*, a drug addict, asking if Troy would run a quick errand with him. Troy scoffed internally.

And Mom thinks I'm in danger…

Half an hour later, Anthony's car pulled up and Troy hopped in. At first, Troy was full of bravado, but then he began to get uneasy; Anthony was driving oddly, fidgeting and sweating profusely. He suddenly veered off the road into a motel parking lot, stammering, "I, I just gotta make a stop, real quick... you, you comin' in?"

Troy shook his head emphatically.

"No way, man—I'm not going in there with you!"

Anthony didn't push further. He nodded nervously, then hurried into the motel. Troy waited impatiently, getting more suspicious by the minute.

Suddenly, a large car raced into the parking lot and screeched into the spot beside Troy. Instinct kicked in, and Troy flung open his door, hitting the other car. He squeezed himself out, adrenaline pumping through him, and took off across the parking lot. His feet sped over the gravel, and he could hear two men cursing behind him. Then came another sound that struck him with terror: *Bang! Bang! Bang!*

Gunshots echoed across the parking lot; Troy ducked and dodged as bullets zipped past his face and hit the ground around him, sending up sparks.

I just gotta get to the trees... I can ma—

Suddenly, searing hot pain sliced through Troy's shoulder. Troy stumbled, flipping through the air and slamming into the asphalt.

Before he could rise, the two men caught up to him and began kicking Troy and screaming obscenities. He struggled, trying to get to his feet, but somehow the bullet in his shoulder had paralyzed his entire right side; he was pinned to the ground and couldn't even lift an arm to protect himself from the blows.

Suddenly, the men stopped. Then, one lifted his gun, and aimed it right at Troy's face.

Troy panicked.

Time seemed to freeze, and moment after moment from Troy's life flashed through his mind: *Nine years old, watching two coffins being lowered into the ground in Port Sulphur, Louisiana... walking up during the altar call in church... 16 years old, yelling at his mom... leaving home for the streets, selling drugs... his mom's tear-stained face, "I never thought you'd turn out like this"... lounging in that old casino, talking with a bunch of drunk men about Heaven...*

Heaven... am I really gonna wake up there when this guy pulls the trigger?

Terror gripped Troy's chest as he stared up powerlessly at the gun ready to spit metal into his skull and end his life.

Is this how it ends?

The man pulled the trigger.

Click.

The gun jammed.

Troy watched in confusion as the man cursed, then turned and ran into the motel. The other assailant stepped forward and began to stomp on Troy viciously, smacking his head and body into the concrete. In his partially paralyzed state, all Troy could do was curl inward, helpless to defend himself against the savage blows.

When the man had finished, leaving Troy in a bloodied heap, his partner came back out of the motel. Troy had lost a lot of blood and was having trouble focusing. But in the distance, he heard sirens and hope sprang alive.

At least these guys are gonna get caught...

Police cars and an ambulance roared into the parking lot, lights blazing. Troy watched in shock as his two attackers didn't run, but instead walked calmly up to the approaching officers. The one with the gun motioned at Troy and said, "Glad you got my call for backup... he was armed, shot at us, then attacked. Trev* finally got him in the shoulder, but he put up quite a fight."

Me shoot? I didn't even bring a gun—

The officer nodded.

"Well done, boys. This fella's got to learn not to mess with undercover cops."

What?

Troy lay bleeding on the ground in shock and total confusion.

The officers thoroughly examined him and discovered several drug packages he had stuffed in his pockets; as Troy was handcuffed and loaded into the ambulance, one of the cops recited, "Troy Gause, you are under arrest for the possession of cocaine and for the attempted murder of two police officers. You have the right to remain silent..."

The words faded as Troy drifted in and out of consciousness.

***

Troy lay in the hospital, his head locked in one position by a neck brace, and his arms and legs handcuffed to the bed, while a police officer sat on the opposite side of the room, monitoring him closely. Troy watched the small television screen in his hospital room in disbelief as his story came out on the news.

"Earlier this week, 21-year-old Troy Gause, an infamous New Orleans drug dealer, was arrested for the attempted murder of two police officers, and could face up to 50 years in prison without parole…"

As he gritted his teeth, Troy angrily slammed his one good hand into his bed, causing the policeman to shift uncomfortably.

That ain't what happened…

The action of slamming his hand into the bed caused pain to radiate through Troy's body, and tears of bitterness leaked from Troy's eyes.

Here I am chained to this bed… I can't go anywhere, I can't fight, I can't talk to anyone, and even if I could, no one would ever believe my story…

Troy clenched his fist in frustration, then winced in pain. His whole body had been badly bruised and battered from the vicious stomping, and worst of all, his right side remained partially paralyzed from the bullet's penetration in his shoulder. While the doctors said he would eventually regain movement, for the time being, Troy was… *not in charge.*

Troy seethed as his mom's words came back to him. Every fiber of his being fought against the idea, but in his current condition, the truth was undeniable.

After several days in the hospital, Troy was transferred to prison. Because of the severity of his injuries, the prison authorities deemed it unsafe to house Troy in the general population where he would be unable to protect himself from other inmates.

So he was instead transported to a one-man suicide cell. As Troy entered the cell, the door slammed behind him, sending echoes up and down the hall. Troy's eyes traveled quickly around the room, taking in his surroundings. A dingy, white, ten-by-ten-foot room, with a steel cot, steel toilet-sink combo, and slot in the wall for food trays. The door was just a seam in the wall and there were no windows, only a harsh white ceiling light—flat to keep prisoners from hanging themselves.

The light never turned off, and Troy lost track of time; he slept when he felt tired, and only knew when it was 7 a.m. because the correctional officer delivered his breakfast plate. He had nothing to do all day but sit and stare at the same white walls; at night his sleep was interrupted by the screams of other suicidal prisoners around him.

Troy, who had once believed himself to be invincible, was now at the mercy of others, utterly dependent and powerless.

***

Three weeks later...

Troy sat crumpled on the floor of the cell, trembling and staring wild-eyed around him.

As he looked down at his limp arm and leg, and then around at the bare, white walls holding him in, Troy felt a crazed desperation well up inside him, a sensation he'd felt only once before in life. His breath came quick and shallow, and he felt like his throat was closing with panic. It took him back to that horrible day which was burned into his memory.

Opening his nine-year-old eyes to murky darkness, trying to breathe... his lungs filling with brackish water... kicking wildly, unsure which way was up... feeling his brother pushing him to the surface... getting pulled into a stranger's boat, his brother and dad slipping away beneath him...

Ever since then, Troy had told himself fiercely that he would never let anything in his life come out of his control again.

Now I can't lift my arm, can't leave this room... I can't even take my own life.

Troy felt rage build up in his chest, and then he collapsed on the cold cement floor, screaming into the deafening silence, "God, how could You let this happen? Why didn't You warn me?"

Troy was startled by the response of a small, gentle voice.

I did warn you... I've always been right here, calling you. But you were living too fast, you weren't listening.

Scenario after scenario began to play back in Troy's head.

Surviving the accident in the Port Sulphur bayou, even though his dad and brother had drowned... countless sermons he had heard in church as a boy growing up... his mom calling to warn him about the setup... the gun jamming right as the trigger was pulled to end his life...

God had been calling, and Troy had ignored Him.

Troy cried out at the ceiling, "I'm listening now, God! I've tried everything... I've tried going straight and getting a job; I've tried women and the club scene; I've tried the streets, selling drugs for fame and money. There's no hope for me, I've tried it all."

You haven't tried Me.

Tears streaked down Troy's bruised face, and he sobbed desperately, "Lord, I wanna try You! I wanna live for You!"

He bowed his head, shaking with hopeless weeping.

"But God—I don't know how. I don't have anything to offer… just this broken life."

I'll take it. Troy, I'll take all of it… and I'll make it new.

Troy's sobs subsided. He looked up at the ceiling. "OK, God. Then—here You go."

Troy had talked about Jesus his whole life and knew all *about* Him, but had never truly *known* Him.

Alone in that cell, Troy felt all of his pain and sorrow and sin be washed away by the blood of the Savior, and for the first time in years, a genuine smile spread across his face. After trying to control God all his life, Troy had finally relinquished his tight-fisted grip and surrendered his life to God.

***

Weeks later, Troy was transferred into the general prison population.

As he took his first steps into his new dorm, Troy stopped in his tracks. Sitting at a table, in a circle of other inmates, was Damion, Troy's top drug runner.

Damion glanced up, and upon seeing Troy, a huge grin of disbelief spread across his face. He quickly put down the book he had been reading aloud and hurried over to grip his friend in a hug.

"Troy! Whatcha doing here? Man, it's so good to see you! It's been a minute—"

Troy laughed with Damion. Then he noticed the book Damion had been reading to the other inmates: a Bible.

Damion laughed at Troy's obvious surprise.

"Hard to believe, isn't it? These guys here are in my Bible study." The men around the table nodded at Troy. "And that Jesus you was always talking about? Man, He saved my life!"

The two men talked for hours, both overjoyed to hear of each other's conversion. Over the next few weeks, Troy joined Damion's Bible study, and the two men encouraged each other and grew in their faith together. Troy could hardly believe the kindness of God to him; Troy now shared a dorm not only with a friend, but also a brother in Christ.

***

Troy smiled as he stepped past the razor-wire fence, feeling warm sunlight hit his face as a free man for the first time in six months. His mom stood by her car waiting, wiping tears from her eyes and wrapped him in her arms.

Through a series of unbelievable miracles, the attempted murder charges had been dropped. An eyewitness at the motel had seen the undercover police officers shoot Troy, unprovoked, and several other testimonies from people in the motel confirmed that the initial police report was false. After a local journalist uncovered the real story the prosecutors offered Troy a plea deal. Troy was free.

But Troy also knew the truth.

Jesus, You've delivered me, in every way. My old life was a prison cell, and I was locked inside, thinking I was in control. I deserved to stay in there forever; but Lord, You hold the keys, and You've set my soul free!

For the first time, someone besides Troy was in charge of his life, and Troy was joyfully following where his Savior led.

***

The beautiful notes of the final hymn rose to the church ceiling, mingling with the morning sunlight from the windows, as the congregation raised their hands in worship.

> *"Through many dangers, toils, and snares,*
> *I have already come;*
> *'Twas grace that brought me safe thus far,*
> *And grace will lead me home."*

The hymn concluded, and the congregation sat down, as the pastor made his way up to the pulpit.

He smiled out at the room, saying, "Good morning everyone, welcome to Cross Community Church at Ames. My name is Troy Gause, and I serve as the lead pastor here." Troy smiled down at his wife of 20 years, Chanel.

Warmth filled his heart as his eyes traveled to his four kids sitting in the front row and his mom sitting next to them.

"We are so happy you're here, and when I say that I truly mean it."

Troy spread his arms wide.

"Any soul is welcome, because every soul needs Jesus. It doesn't matter who you are, or where you're from. Jesus took me how I was, and made me new; I know He can do the same for you. Just bring your broken life; He'll take it.

"Today, we will be looking at John 8, starting in verse 36—'So if the Son sets you free, you will be free indeed…'"

Bibles opened all over the room as Troy began his sermon.

7

A DOUBLE LIFE

JEFF PARKER

Playing cards, cash, and colored chips flew across countless tables all over Las Vegas; but at one table, a man was making a choice that would change his life.

Jeff held the company credit card in his pocket. His friends chatted around him as they finished dinner, unaware of the internal battle taking place. Out of the corner of his eye, Jeff could see playing cards being dealt at another table; Jeff's mind raced.

I don't have enough cash left to keep playing, but I could use my company credit card to cover the entire bill for everyone at the meal, and then pocket the cash everyone else threw in for their part...

Jeff's conscience burned within him.

Don't do it, don't give in... it's not worth it...

Pulling out the company credit card, Jeff quickly swiped it. He shoved $400 cash into his pocket, then walked off to find a blackjack table.

No big deal, I'll pay the company back as soon as I get home... nobody has to know...

***

Twelve years earlier...

Eighteen-year-old Jeff Parker sat down in the church office, twisting his hands nervously. He had become a Christian a few years prior and had a good relationship with his youth pastor, who sat across from Jeff and smiled kindly at him.

"Now, you said there was something you wanted to talk about?"

Jeff looked down, shuffling his feet. "Yes sir." Jeff cleared his throat. "Well, um—"

Tell him everything, confess it all... Jeff cleared his throat nervously.

"You remember my girlfriend, Alicia*, right? Well, it may have seemed like we had a godly relationship but... I... we made out a few times... well actually, a lot... a lot of kissing and stuff... And it was the same with my other girlfriend, Kaitlyn*, we acted foolishly."

"I see," the pastor said soberly. "Well, I want to commend you, Jeff, for confessing; that takes courage. In 1 John 1:9 it says 'If we confess our sins, he is faithful and just to forgive us our sins and to cleanse us from all unrighteousness.'"

After offering some more counsel and encouragement to Jeff, the pastor looked across the desk and asked, "Is there anything else you would like to tell me?"

Jeff, you did a lot more than just make out...

The gentle voice pressed, and Jeff opened his mouth, total confession on his tongue. But then another voice, low and crafty, whispered, *What will he think of you? What will the church think of you... when they hear you were sleeping with those girls...*

Jeff's mouth snapped shut. "No, sir. That's everything."

The dark voice inside him had won. Jeff didn't know it, but shackles of half-confession had wrapped around him, chaining him down in a darkness that would enslave him for years to come.

Years passed, and Jeff eventually graduated college, and married Stacey, a faithful believer. The young couple settled down in Dallas, Texas, and began attending Watermark Community Church. The Parkers fell in love with the church and quickly became members, joined a community group, and grew close with their small group leaders, Rob and Haley Thomas, a young couple passionate for the Lord.

Jeff was drawn to the vulnerability they exhibited in confessing their sin. He was still gripped by shame over the sexual sin in his teens, but had become adept at compartmentalizing it and hiding behind his Christian façade.

And now Jeff had another dark secret: pornography.

I can deal with it on my own... what would happen if I told?

***

"This is the message we have heard from him and proclaim to you, that God is light, and in him is no darkness at all."

Rob looked up from his Bible, around the church community group.

"What do you all think 1 John 1:5 teaches us?"

During the discussion, Jeff nodded along; but the verse kept replaying in his head, *no darkness at all...*

Later that week Jeff took Rob out to lunch, knowing what he had to do. He looked up from his meal.

"Rob... I've never told anyone this before." Jeff shifted in his seat uncomfortably.

"But, I really want to come clean. I—I slept with a couple of girlfriends in high school... several times. I've never told anyone... not even Stacey."

Now confess the porn...

"I also—"

The other dark voice inside him hissed, *You just confessed the big stuff; preserve your current reputation!*

"—used to struggle with pornography."

You're downplaying it; confess everything, Jeff.

Jeff kept his eyes downcast and remained silent. Rob put a hand on his shoulder.

"You did the right thing by confessing, Jeff, that's what a faithful man of God does. You need to tell Stacey."

That night, as Jeff finished telling his wife what he told Rob, she stared at him in disbelief. "But I *asked* you! Multiple times while we were dating... you lied to me?"

Jeff couldn't meet her gaze.

"I—I was ashamed of the truth."

Over the next few weeks, Rob and Haley visited Jeff and Stacey frequently to support and encourage them. One night, after Rob and Haley had left, Stacey asked, her voice strained with emotion, "Jeff—are you still holding anything back?"

"No. That's... everything."

The dark voice in Jeff's head laughed.

***

Around this time, Texas Hold 'Em Poker was becoming popular.

Jeff had always been good at poker; however, occasional games with friends soon began to grow into something he couldn't control. He started gambling online anonymously and at strange hours. Those close to Jeff were all aware he was playing but had no idea how much it consumed him, or how much money he was betting.

Meanwhile, big changes were happening for Jeff. Rob had launched his own small business, Igniter Media, which provided media resources for churches. Rob was full of ideas about how Igniter could serve Christian communities in new ways but realized he needed help, so Rob invited Jeff to quit his job as an accountant and join Igniter Media.

A few months passed and Igniter Media began to expand. The job felt like a perfect fit for Jeff's skill set, and eventually, he became vice president. But gradually,

Jeff realized his role was outpacing his spiritual maturity. He was leading others, and hearing miraculous stories, while he still struggled with pornography, and his Bible sat virtually untouched. And many nights, after Stacey fell asleep, Jeff slid out of bed, tiptoed into the living room, and started up his computer to gamble the night away. And since his nighttime activities were already shrouded in secrecy, it became all too easy to slip deeper into pornography usage.

***

"Today we will be focusing on 1 John 1:6, which says, 'If we say we have fellowship with him while we walk in darkness, we lie and do not practice the truth.'"

Jeff hardly heard the rest of the pastor's sermon, and later, as he walked out of church, he couldn't ignore the undeniable parallel to his own life.

I say I love the Lord... but I'm so deep in darkness... I'm living a lie...

That week, when Jeff attended his community group's gathering for men, he knew what he had to do. Jeff looked around the circle of men, and his confession with Rob years ago flashed through his mind. Rob wasn't there since he now belonged to a different community group, yet Jeff knew it was important to be vulnerable with these men too. Jeff cleared his throat.

"Umm... guys, I—" Sweat trickled down his forehead. "I need to confess some things to you all, that I've been hiding."

Now's your chance… lay it all out there… The gentle voice urged, but the other voice shrieked, *No! They don't need to know everything…*

Jeff swallowed, pushing down the hot feeling building in his chest.

"I've been… playing some poker, as you guys know, and gambling. I—I think it's gotten a bit out of hand. I might be idolizing it too much… I wanted to confess that, and get your thoughts."

The soft voice inside Jeff whispered sorrowfully, *Jeff… you know it's so much worse than just "a bit out of hand." And you didn't say anything about your pornography addiction…*

The men around the living room offered wise counsel, making sure Jeff would confess to Stacey as well, which he did; but only what he had told them. They advised him strongly to stop playing entirely, and Jeff knew their counsel was right. He promised he would quit, and for the next several months he kept his word.

The dark voice whispered, *See, Jeff? No need to confess it all and ruin your reputation…*

***

"I regret to inform you, Mrs. Parker, that you are infected with an STD, a sexually transmitted disease, most likely from a third party."

The doctor glanced briefly at Jeff, as he and Stacey sat in stunned silence.

Jeff had already confessed the sexual sin during his teenage years to Stacey, but that did nothing to ease his shame and embarrassment. This didn't match the reputation he had built for himself. He fidgeted through the community group meeting when they told their closest friends and left Stacey to tell her parents the news alone.

Late the next night, Jeff snuck into the living room and went online to play a game of poker. He felt shame over the sin in his past and was looking for something, anything, to help him drown out the guilt.

He vowed to keep this new round of gambling a secret; no one had to know anything.

I can control it, he thought.

But Jeff began secretly indulging night after night, and he couldn't deny what was happening in his soul as he willfully wandered into sin.

***

"Hey Jeff! So, your b-day's coming up, and some of the fellas were wondering if you're up for a weekend trip to Vegas to celebrate—let me know what you think!"

Jeff read the text, then pocketed his phone.

Nobody knows I've been gambling online again, so it's fine…

As far as Stacey knew, Jeff hadn't touched a poker game for almost two years. Together, he and Stacey agreed he could go on the guys trip, but should take only $500 cash with him, to spend however he wanted.

And so, leaving all his personal credit cards behind, Jeff flew with some of his college buddies to Las Vegas, aptly known as "Sin City." The trip slipped away quickly, as did Jeff's funds. On the last night, the group went out for dinner and a game of blackjack, and Jeff had only $60 left, enough to pay for his meal, but not enough to keep playing. Yet his hands still itched for the glossy cards and a pile of chips.

Aware he still had his Igniter Media credit card with him, he realized he could quietly cover the entire meal for everyone with the company credit card, pocket the $400 cash everyone else had thrown in to pay for dinner, and keep playing for the rest of the night.

I can pay back Igniter when I get home…

As his friends watched on, never assuming anything was wrong, Jeff swiped his card, paying for everyone's meals, and grabbed the wad of bills. By the end of the night, Jeff had made double what he had pocketed during dinner.

But as he walked out into the black night, set ablaze with garish neon, guilt twisted in his gut.

I just stole from my company—there's no going back now. I've reached the point of no return.

When Jeff got home, he quietly repaid Igniter and kept his mouth shut. Since he held oversight of Igniter's finances, Jeff didn't have to run his transactions by anyone. He continued to gamble online secretly, using whatever personal money Stacey wouldn't notice.

One night, in the darkened living room, lit only by the glow of the computer, Jeff stared at his nearly empty personal gambling account. He knew he should shut down the laptop and go to bed.

Just one more game…

Before he knew it, Jeff had logged into the Igniter bank account.

I'll pay it back as soon as the game is over...

Even though Jeff sat in complete silence, the voice inside of him seemed loud as it warned him, pleaded with him. Jeff quickly clicked "transfer," giving the voice no time to convince him to do otherwise.

What Jeff had told himself would be a one-time exception in Vegas began to happen almost every time he gambled secretly. And while he usually tried to repay Igniter promptly, gradually, his repayments became more sporadic.

By the end of that year, Jeff had stolen $5,000 from Igniter Media.

Before long, he began using company money not just for gambling, but to purchase sports tickets for resale and to cover sundry personal expenses and entertainment. As the years sped by, Jeff told himself he would pay it back, but eventually, he could no longer justify his out-of-control spending and paying back all of the money became impossible.

It was exhausting, leading such a double life. On the outside, Jeff was vice president of a Christian media company, a faithful husband and father of two, a Christ-follower and an example in the church. But in the dark, Jeff was a hardened, lying man, addicted to pornography and gambling, and stealing from his best friend's company to fund his sin.

***

A cold wind whistled past, as Jeff stood in front of the ATM—numb, chilled to his very core. He looked down at the company check in his hand, then scanned the parking lot, expecting the police to roar up any minute to arrest him.

Don't do it, Jeff...

Sliding in the check, Jeff hesitated, then tapped the button to transfer the money into his private account.

The check was made out for $50,000.

Jeff hadn't intended to become a white-collar criminal and betray his best friend, but the years of choosing to conceal the full truth had given increasing strength to the chains which yanked him deeper and deeper into sin.

And now, the contrast between his two lives could hardly be more pronounced. He made sure his family was at church every Sunday, he attended community group faithfully, and was constantly talking about the importance of creating quality media for churches and pastors that would reach the lost and care for the flock. But when no one was looking, Jeff's actions told a completely different story. As the years passed and his debt to Igniter continued to pile up over his head, Jeff's two lives were tearing him apart.

Finally, alone in his office one day, Jeff wrote out a list, detailing who he wanted to be:

- An Ephesians 5 husband…
- A 2 Timothy 2 worker…
- A Psalm 127 father…

Jeff looked helplessly at what he had written. *I could never become this man… I'm too far gone…*

But something in his heart couldn't bear to throw the list away. Jeff folded it and shoved it deep into his backpack.

***

It was January 18, 2015, and Jeff sat in a packed room of business leaders.

With Igniter growing so rapidly, Rob had decided that he and Jeff should attend a Business Mastery Conference in Florida. Rob now sat beside Jeff, furiously scribbling notes, pausing only to grin excitedly at his friend.

He doesn't even know what I'm doing to Igniter… to him…

Jeff blinked hard, pushing his thoughts away. The 65-year-old Texan who was humorously discussing debits and credits on stage, suddenly stopped, his voice echoing through the auditorium.

"Y'all don't know this, but once, I hated who I was."

Jeff's head snapped up.

"My wife and family hated me, and I hated myself—I was at the end of my rope."

The speaker went on to share some of the sin that had haunted him for years, and Jeff leaned forward in his seat.

"I was terrified of what I had become. But then I had a thought that terrified me more: what if I met the man God intended me to be, and I had never become that man?"

A silence filled the room as Jeff sat back, mind reeling, and his mind went immediately to the crumpled list buried in his backpack.

That's me... I hate who I am—who I've become.

That night, in his hotel room, Jeff pulled from his backpack the faded list he had written 15 months earlier. The words he had written were rubbed out entirely in some places and rips were starting to form along some of the fold lines. Jeff didn't need to look at the list anymore; the words were etched in his memory. They often replayed in his mind, in a haunting, indicting tone that made Jeff shudder and crumple the list, returning it to its place in the bottom of his backpack.

But tonight was different. Tonight, Jeff's eyes lingered over the words he had written, and instead of feeling self-loathing and guilt, he felt a tiny glimmer of hope. His thoughts returned to the man at the conference who had hated himself and his story of how Jesus had changed him.

Reaching for his Bible, and flipping to the Gospels, Jeff began to read story after story of Jesus interacting with sinners. The woman at the well, the demon-possessed man, the prostitute who had washed Jesus' feet with her precious ointment... Zacchaeus. Jeff stopped short. Zacchaeus... the man who had stolen from numerous people.

"Today salvation has come to this house…" Jeff read the words from Luke 19 out loud. "For the Son of Man came to seek and to save the lost."

Lord, I feel lost, like I've been wandering for a long time…

He held up the faded list.

God, I want to be this man, the man You want me to be—but I'm scared.

Jeff took out a pen and paper, and wrote two columns labeled "pros" and "cons." Beneath each, he wrote what would happen if he confessed. If he confessed *everything*.

A few minutes later, Jeff sat back. His eyes blurred with hopeless tears, as he reread the cons column: *You will devastate your best friend, your family, your wife… you could tear down Igniter… you might go to jail… expose yourself for the man you are…*

Then he turned to the other column: *You will be free.*

Jeff felt his heart would burst with longing. He glanced down at the worn list describing the man he so desired to be, a free man.

Then, he felt the Lord gently whisper, *Jeff, this man confesses. And he confesses everything.*

The verse that Jeff's youth pastor had shared with him all those years ago resurfaced in Jeff's mind: *If we confess our sins, he is faithful and just to forgive us our sins and to cleanse us from all unrighteousness.*

Jeff put his head in his hands.

I want to, Lord—I just don't know if I can…

The next day, seated next to Rob on an airplane headed home, Jeff listlessly opened his iPad, and selected *The Cost of Discipleship* by Dietrich Bonhoeffer.

I've been meaning to read this for years...

He began the first chapter, which compared the difference between cheap grace and costly grace. Bonhoeffer described cheap grace as something believers extend to themselves, requiring no confession, no repentance, and no Savior. But costly grace was what Jesus bought for sinners; a grace found at the foot of the cross, that sinners must fall on again and again; costly because it requires the courage to admit they need it.

Jeff turned his head toward the window, tears streaming down his face.

Man... I've been hoping for cheap grace. I've been wanting Jesus to wash away all my sins, without ever having to acknowledge all of them. Here I am, calling myself a Christ-follower, sitting next to my best friend whom I've stolen six figures of money from...

Rob put a hand on Jeff's shoulder.

"Jeff, are you ok?"

Jeff nodded, and with a concerned look, Rob returned to his notes.

Hands trembling, unable to believe what he was doing, Jeff typed out a group text to the men in his community group.

"I need you all to meet with me as soon as I get back. I've got some life-changing things to confess, and I'm going to need help to walk through what comes next."

That very day, January 19, 2015, for the first time in his life, Jeff confessed *everything*.

The secret gambling, embezzlement, and pornography usage, he laid it all out to his brothers in Christ. Seven years of hidden sin, six figures of financial thievery, and a lifetime of half-confessions; he confessed it all.

Later that afternoon, accompanied by the men in his community group, Jeff confessed to Stacey. She sat in stunned silence for a long time. Then she met her husband's gaze, eyes wet with tears, and said softly, "Jeff, I am not without hope. Jesus will carry us through this too."

That evening, the Parkers sat in Rob and Haley's living room and, with their community group present, Jeff confessed everything. Rob was shocked and saddened, but at the end of the evening he solemnly thanked Jeff, saying they could go over details another night.

As Jeff lay his head on the pillow that night, physically and emotionally exhausted, he felt the Lord whisper, *My son, today you have been faithful. Rest now, for the sleep of the righteous is satisfying.*

Jeff woke the next day from the first restful night of sleep he had had in years. He was fired by Rob later that day and was unsure if Igniter would press charges or try to prosecute him for his actions, which would have been well within their rights to do. There was a hard road ahead of Jeff, but all was out in broad daylight, and he was finally free.

Over the following months, the Parkers' church community surrounded the family with encouragement and care. One man offered to oversee the Parkers' financial situation for the time being, and Jeff gratefully surrendered all his credit cards, account numbers, and bank logins. At the same time, Jeff began praying passionately and devouring God's Word, reading the Bible for hours on end.

Rob asked Jeff to perform a full audit of what he had stolen, and Jeff readily complied, giving himself no mercy. In the end, he produced a 44-page report, revealing that he had stolen $250,000 from Igniter, while only repaying approximately $150,000.

Jeff was devastated, staring at the ugly audit.

How is this forgivable?

Jeff glanced over to his Bible, and his eyes fell onto the verses he had read just that morning in Ezekiel 33:15–16:

> *"...if the wicked restores the pledge, gives back what he has taken by robbery, and walks in the statutes of life, not doing injustice, he shall surely live; he shall not die. None of the sins that he has committed shall be remembered against him. He has done what is just and right; he shall surely live."*

Jeff's eyes filled with tears, *Lord, I'm utterly dependent on Your grace. Please, help me to repay the company, and let any shame over my sin only point to Your power to save.*

***

Through a mixture of odd jobs, liquidating assets, and selling off college funds, Jeff was able to repay Igniter back fully by the end of 2015.

A year after his initial confession, Jeff sat across the table from Rob to seek forgiveness for a number of things: the actual dollar amount he had stolen, his betrayal of Rob's friendship as well as the hurt he had caused Rob's family, and the ways he had endangered the company.

"Jeff," Rob said thoughtfully, "I've already forgiven you. Your repentance has made it easier on me, so thank you. We thought about prosecuting you, but in the end, we decided to give you a chance to pay the company back, which you did much more quickly than we expected."

In keeping with the fruit of repentance, Jeff became open with others about his experience living a double life and the freedom he found through full confession. Eventually, Jeff joined his church's staff to lead their biblical recovery ministry.

Jeff is quick to point out that his complete transformation is the result of God's grace in his life and not his own strength. In 2023, in a redemptive turn of events, Rob invited Jeff to rejoin Igniter Media as their Chief Business Development Officer, where Jeff continues to work today.

CONCLUSION

The stories in this book are just the tip of the iceberg.

Take a look at the Bible, and you'll find them everywhere, stories that boggle our finite human minds.

A childless man is promised he will have a son; more than that, he's promised an entire nation will come from him. His 90-year-old wife conceives and gives birth to a son, eventually leading to the entire nation of Israel. What is impossible… happens.

A people group has been miraculously rescued from generations of slavery and is traveling to the Promised Land. Men, women, and children, all painstakingly making their way through the desert. When the Egyptian army appears to recapture them and take them back into captivity, they're trapped. Pharoah's soldiers behind them and the Red Sea in front of them… there's no way to escape. Instead, in an event that defies all forces of nature, the sea splits in half, and the Israelites walk across on dry land.

A humble, young Jewish woman winds up becoming queen of the Persian Empire and, shortly after, a decree is issued which will annihilate her people. The timing of the events is unbelievable. The young queen has been positioned perfectly to advocate for her people, and, as a result, Israel is spared from total genocide.

A giant slain with just a stone, lions' mouths stopped, thousands fed from a few simple loaves and fishes, a mere human able to walk on water, blind eyes opened, lame legs jumping, and the dead raised to life...

These stories, incredible as they are, represent only a handful of examples, just a few drops of water in the vast ocean of miracles and astounding stories spilling over from the world's greatest book.

And the stories don't end with the Bible; the whole landscape of history is filled with countless more of these spectacular encounters.

Men like George Müller, who cared for more than 10,000 orphans without ever fundraising a single penny, instead fully relying on prayer. Women like Amy Carmichael, who was able to disguise herself as an Indian woman—because of her brown eyes which she had once despised—and rescue over 1,000 girls enslaved in Hindu temples. John Newton, a slave trader turned hymn writer. Corrie ten Boom, a survivor of a Nazi prison camp, who forgave her enemies.

These kinds of stories are still being written today, millions of them, all over the globe. When we encounter them, our incredulous thoughts immediately protest,

CONCLUSION

"Those sort of things just don't happen anymore..." And yet, the seven stories you've just read in this book speak for themselves.

How could a girl like Laura Perry—steeped in the transgender lifestyle for a decade, all the time growing more hopeless on her quest to find fulfillment as a man—suddenly turn away from all she had lived for... and discover joy as a daughter of God?

Who could ever dream up the rich irony threaded throughout Troy Gause's life? Called "Church Boy" by his friends, often found in the pews of a church, feeling smug in his ability to simultaneously play the part of "religious"... and drug dealer. But after many dramatic twists and turns, Troy is in the church again—this time in the pulpit as a pastor and a passionate follower of Jesus Christ.

Such radical transformations seem completely implausible, and yet, these stories aren't simply nice sentiments or a sort of feel-good fairy tale. They're reality.

They challenge us to look beyond their human characters and leave us instead wondering about their Author.

None of these stories happened by chance. Each one has been skillfully crafted by the God of the universe, breathed out through His heart of love for humanity. "God stories", as we often call them, are uniquely compelling because they have been written with more than mere pen and paper, but instead with the very blood of Jesus Christ.

Incredibly, this is the same God who is, at this moment, writing *your* story.

"In your book were written, every one of them, the days that were formed for me, when as yet there was none of them." (Psalm 139:16)

All of your days have been written by God in detail, before you even existed.

The dark, stormy days, and the bright, sunny ones. The seasons of mind-numbing boredom and the moments of fast-paced exhilaration. The joys of new life and the heartache of loss. From young to old, rich to poor, healthy to sick… Each of your days is a loving stroke of His pen, all of the pieces coming together in ways more beautiful than you could ever imagine, to craft a perfectly magnificent story of His glory.

Do you find that difficult to believe? Then take courage, and find faith in all that He promises you!

If your story feels hopeless, God reassures you, "I know the plans I have for you… plans for welfare and not for evil, to give you a future and a hope." (Jeremiah 29:11)

If you're facing monsters and dragons and your story feels terrifying, know that God is exhorting you, *commanding* you, "Do not be frightened, and do not be dismayed, for the Lord your God is with you wherever you go." (Joshua 1:9)

Maybe you're stuck in the middle of a long and winding chapter, one which appears to be going absolutely nowhere. Don't give up! His goodness is certainly present, though sometimes hidden in seemingly endless pages. Wait for the Lord and for the end of the story! (Psalm 27:13-14)

Maybe your faith has faded and you're worried that God has given up on your story. Crumpled it up and tossed it aside in exchange for a fresh start with someone else, someone more worthy than yourself. Remember the story of the Prodigal Son. God is eager, longing, to wrap you in the arms of His loving embrace. So turn and run home to your loving Father!

If pain and suffering have overtaken your life and you're worried your story will never have a "happily ever after," God is gently lifting your eyes from the dismal here and now to glorious eternity whispering, "With Me, there are pleasures forevermore." (Psalm 16:11, paraphrase)

And if you've spent your whole life trying to pry the pen out of God's hand, desperate to write your own story, cease your striving and hear God's declaration, "For as the heavens are higher than the earth, so are my ways higher than your ways and my thoughts than your thoughts." (Isaiah 55:9)

The sin in all of our hearts has destined our tales to be nightmarish, horror stories of the worst sort. And no matter how good we try to be, we can never make our stories good; sin engulfs our hearts with relentless darkness, condemning us to eternal death.

But God allowed His Son, Jesus, to voluntarily suffer punishment for the sins of any who would trust in Him for salvation. He rose back to life to prove that he has victory over death and offer you hope of a life to come.

He did that so that, in the end, your story isn't actually *your* story at all but a story of *Him*—Him rescuing you from the greedy tentacles of sin and Hell, turning your heart from darkness to light, and giving you a glorious future forever with Him.

Whatever part of the story you find yourself in right now, lift your eyes to the Author, and trust that beauty is flowing from His Heavenly pen. Watch expectantly as He continues to write, and find that the story He is creating is far, far better than anything for which you could ever dare to hope.

— *Paul & Sarah Hastings*

CONTRIBUTORS

Hannah Overton continues to share the gospel and minister to those in prison. She and her husband started Syndeo Ministries, which is dedicated to helping women in prison. Today, Syndeo reaches out to thousands of inmates. To learn more visit SyndeoMinistries.com.

Carol Richardson went to be with her Savior in 2004 and **Don Richardson** followed in 2018. Their deaths were mourned by thousands around the globe but the work they began continues to this day and is preserved at PeaceChildLegacy.com. You can read more about Don and Carol's time with the Sawi in their book *Peace Child*.

Laura Perry Smalts and her husband established Eden's Redemption as a way to help others understand God's design for gender. You can learn more at EdensRedemption.org and read a fuller account of Laura's experience in her book *Transgender to Transformed*.

Brian Birdwell was elected to the Texas State Senate in 2010. His 9/11 experience is written about in more detail in his book *Refined by Fire*.

Carol Everett established The Heidi Group in 1995 to help women facing unplanned pregnancies. Learn more at HeidiGroup.org and read Carol's full story in her book *Blood Money*.

Troy Gause leads the homeless ministry, Church Without Walls. You can find out more about the church he pastors, Cross Community Church at Ames, at CrossCommunity.net.

Jeff Parker now runs Double Edged Notes, a company that produces journals and distributes free Bibles to countries closed to the gospel. Learn more at DoubleEdgedNotes.com.

If you enjoyed reading the stories in this book, then please check out our free podcast, **Compelled**.

We use gripping, immersive storytelling to bring Christian testimonies to life and have released over 100 stories (and counting!) that illustrate God's power.

Available anywhere podcasts can be found.

Learn more at **CompelledPodcast.com**

If you have been impacted by the stories in this book then let us know by emailing **contact@compelledpodcast.com**

More books from 10Publishing

Resources that point to Jesus

Are you 100% sure you want to be an agnostic?
ANDREW SACH & JONATHAN GEMMELL

Making Sense of Life
MICHAEL OTS

Have You Ever Wondered?
Edited by ANDY BANNISTER & GAVIN MATTHEWS

To find out more visit:
10ofthose.com

10 Publishing
a division of 10ofthose.com